"*Please Seek the Truth* is a must read for anyone seeking honest answers to eternal matters. Tony in his appeal to the unbeliever to look honestly at the Christian faith has captured the appeal of the Apostle Paul, 'to speak the truth and do it in love' (Eph. 4:15)."

~Travis Tobin
Pastor, First Baptist Church
Garner, North Carolina

"A book that will reach many with the simple message of salvation in Jesus Christ in our present complicated world. The Christian heart of the author is found on every page."

~Tom Jordan, D.Min., Ph.D.
Senior Pastor, First Baptist Church, Epworth, Georgia
Director of Toccoa Falls College, Epworth, Georgia
Professor of Bible and Western Thought and Culture

PLEASE
SEEK
THE
Truth

PLEASE
SEEK
THE
Truth

Overcoming Roadblocks to Christianity

TONY BLALOCK

TATE PUBLISHING & *Enterprises*

The opinions expressed by the author are not necessarily those of Tate Publishing, LLC.

Published by Tate Publishing & Enterprises, LLC
127 E. Trade Center Terrace | Mustang, Oklahoma 73064 USA
1.888.361.9473 | www.tatepublishing.com

Tate Publishing is committed to excellence in the publishing industry. The company reflects the philosophy established by the founders, based on Psalm 68:11,
"The Lord gave the word and great was the company of those who published it."

Book design copyright © 2007 by Tate Publishing, LLC. All rights reserved.
Cover design by Isaiah McKee
Interior design by Elizabeth A. Mason

Published in the United States of America

ISBN: 978-1-60247-868-8

1. Christian Living   2. Spiritual Growth
3. Contemplative Life
07.08.27

DEDICATION

I dedicate this book to my Lord and Savior, Jesus Christ. Thank you for paying the price for my sins. Thank you for the joy and value you bring to my life. Thank you for your love and friendship. Thank you for your guidance in writing this book.

ACKNOWLEDGMENTS

I want to thank my wife and best friend, Beverly, for her love and support throughout our twenty-five years of marriage. Thank you for your encouragement as I wrote this book and for not laughing when I first told you I felt led to write a book. It still seems unbelievable, doesn't it? Thank you for reading the book several times to catch my mistakes and for your suggestions.

Kevin and Troy, thank you for being such great sons and friends. Thanks for your understanding as I have monopolized the computer a lot lately and also for helping me edit the book.

I want to thank my parents, David and Ethel, for demonstrating to me what unconditional love is. Thank you for all of the sacrifices you have made for me and Jerry. I hope you understand how much I appreciate the fact that you have always been there for me.

I have had three very special pastors in my life: Dr. Tom Jordan, Rev. Travis Tobin, and Rev. Don Chasteen. Dr. Jordan introduced me to Christ and all three of these men have been tremendous role models in what it means to love and serve Jesus.

My Sunday School class, "The Seekers", at Ridgecrest Baptist Church has been such a blessing in my life. I am so thankful for each and every person that God has led to our class and the sweet fellowship that we have. Thank you for your encouragement and prayers as I wrote this book.

I want to give a special thank you to Rick and Fran Tucker. Your encouragement and support have been such an inspiration to me and I am truly thankful to God for your witness and friendship.

I also want to thank the following Christian authors whose books have been such an influence in my life: Henry Blackaby, David Jeremiah, Anne Graham Lotz, Max Lucado, John MacArthur, Beth Moore, Bob Mumford, Charles Stanley, Charles Swindoll, Rick Warren, and Bruce Wilkinson. Most of my days begin with reading the Bible. I have truly been blessed, encouraged, and enlightened as I have ended a lot of my days by reading one of your books.

Finally, I want to thank Tate Publishing. I had no idea how to get a book published and I feel God worked to lead me to you. Thank you for willingness to work with an unknown person and for helping me to publish this message that I felt very strongly God wanted me to share.

Contents

FOREWORD

Please Seek the Truth is one man's journey from a life-style of comfortable silence as a believer to an intentional lifestyle of compassionately sharing the peace, joy, and hope one can have as the result of an intimate walk with Jesus Christ. Throughout my ministry as a pastor, I have been trained and then allowed to equip others how to deal with the objections people share as to why they will not consider Jesus Christ. The goal of overcoming these barriers is personally shared in a non-threatening way through the words of a tender-hearted author who is experiencing first-hand the fulfillment Jesus provides.

As I read the words of the author, the sincerity of his message stirred my heart and challenged me to be constantly aware of the loneliness, hurt, disappointment, and confusion people around me are confronted with on a daily basis. You cannot read his words without giving a serious listening ear to what comes from his heart.

Take this book into your hands. Find a quiet place. Read it carefully. You will discover truths that will be refreshing and comforting as you continue in your journey.

~Donald R. Chasteen
Senior Pastor, Ridgecrest Baptist Church

INTRODUCTION

Making a discovery can be a very exciting thing. It does not even have to be something major. For example, I have seen people get really excited about a new television show and could not wait to tell their friends. Others have discovered a new product that worked well for them and felt they needed to share the product with other people so they could also enjoy the same benefits.

I made the greatest discovery of my life in 1982. I started attending a church with my girl friend who later became my wife. I remember listening to the pastor's message Sunday after Sunday and feeling he was speaking directly to me. It made sense to me that God is a perfect and holy God who will not tolerate sin. It was very easy to understand that every man is a sinner and I knew for sure that I was a sinner. My sin, like every man's sin, creates a separation from God. How can this separation be overcome? What could possibly bridge the gap between my sinfulness and the one and only Holy God? The answer would have to come from God. His solution was to allow Jesus, His Son, to come to Earth and live a perfect life and then be sacrificed to pay for the sins of each person. In order for someone to then have their sins paid for they have to accept Jesus and acknowledge Him as Lord. Finally, one Sunday, I decided to ignore the temptation to delay my decision once again and I accepted Jesus. The last twenty-five years have been a time of learning about Jesus and His love for me.

I believe in God and I believe the Bible is the perfect word of God. I believe there is a Heaven and there is a Hell. I also believe that Jesus Christ is the only way to Heaven because that is what the Bible says. However, since I have these beliefs, I also have a burden. I realize that people all around me have not accepted Christ. Since I believe that Christ is the only way to Heaven, I am very concerned about the eternal destiny of any person who has not accepted Jesus Christ. Just as I felt a tremendous pull to Christ in 1982, I feel a strong sense today that God wants me to get busy about sharing the good news and the critically important message of salvation through Christ.

My purpose in writing this book is to address some of the issues that I sense are keeping people from being receptive to Christ. I feel like some people are simply ignoring the message that Christ came to Earth to die for people's sins so that we can go to Heaven. Others are turned off by the hypocritical actions they see from Christians. Some people have convinced themselves that Christianity is all about money, and churches simply want more people in order to get more money. I hope to address these three issues along with several others.

I have stressed my beliefs and no one should believe something simply because I do. I hope you will sense I have no desire to force my beliefs on anyone. My desire is that this book will help motivate some people to pursue the truth for themselves. Ultimately, the only thing that should matter to you is whether the statement that Jesus is the only way to Heaven is true or not. Even if someone lives to be a 100 years old their life on this Earth is a very short time compared to eternity. Don't you owe it to yourself to discover the truth?

I know the many benefits I have experienced by accepting Christ and I truly want everyone to experience the joy and peace that He provides in this life. It is also an amazing comfort to have the full assurance in your heart that once you experience death on this Earth that Jesus and God are waiting for you in Heaven.

I sincerely hope you will read this book with an open mind and heart. I trust you will sense my genuine concern for people and their eternal destiny. If you are not a Christian, my prayer is this book will cause you to reflect and pursue your answer to what I think is the most important question of life: Who is Jesus to me?

REJECTING JESUS BY IGNORING HIM

One of my favorite television shows when I was growing up was *Hogan's Heroes*. This show was about a POW camp in Germany during World War II. The head of the camp was the bumbling Colonel Klink. The POW's were constantly doing things to help the Allies' war cause. They had tunnels to leave the camp in order to perform secret missions such as blowing up bridges or rescuing other soldiers.

One of the German sergeants in the camp was Sgt. Schultz. He would stumble on the POW's doing something they should not be doing. Instead of punishing them, he would just ignore what they were doing. He would walk away after making a discovery and say, "I hear nothing, I see nothing, I know nothing." Sgt. Schultz did not want to be bothered, so he chose to ignore something when it was his duty to address the situation.

I am afraid many people are taking Sgt. Schultz's approach in terms of addressing the question of who is Jesus Christ. They do not want to be bothered or take any chance of upsetting their world, so the decision is made to just ignore the subject altogether. Ignoring an issue many times leads to disaster because some issues will not simply go away and they must be addressed at some point. One issue that will definitely not go away is what happens to us after we die.

Our church recently went through the 40 *Days of Purpose* based on Rick Warren's book, *The Purpose Driven Life*. One of the major areas of shame in my life is the knowledge that I have not shared the good news of Jesus Christ like I should have. I think part of my issue is the fact that I am a very non-confrontational person. I want everyone to get along and I hate it when I feel friction with another person. Therefore, I tend to keep quiet and not "rock the boat" because I do not want to make people, and to be honest myself, feel uncomfortable. Going through the 40 day journey I realized I should not keep ignoring the fact that so many people around me do not know Jesus Christ. I felt a tremendous sense of responsibility to change this aspect in my life and attempt to reach people for Christ before it is too late.

My hope is people who are not Christians will read this book and be motivated to genuinely seek the truth about Jesus. Since they are reading a book they will not have to answer anyone right away. It appears to me many times when someone is being witnessed to about Christ they are really uncomfortable and just want the experience to be over with. Their mind seems to be racing and often they are not really listening very much because they are wondering what to say in order to end the conversation.

The majority of this book will address several of the specific issues which appear to be roadblocks for many people in considering the message of salvation offered by Jesus Christ. The good news is when someone has a specific concern or concerns keeping them from Christ, there are points that can be made for them to consider because they are at least willing to address the subject.

However, some people have decided they just do not want to be bothered by any of this "religious stuff" and are intent on going through life ignoring the issue altogether. If you are one of these people I hope you will decide that ignoring the issues of whether there is a God, what happens to you after you die and the significance of Jesus Christ are matters that just cannot be ignored any longer.

A group of Samaritans once told another Samaritan woman:

> They said to the woman, "We no longer believe just because of what you said: now we have heard for ourselves, and we know that this man really is the Savior of the world."
>
> (John 4:42)

The point is you must make a conscious decision that you want to seek the truth for yourself. It is an individual choice that every person must make. By ignoring the subject you are in fact making the choice against Christ. Is that really the choice you want to make?

God makes a very special promise in the Old Testament book of Jeremiah. He was writing to the people of Israel during one of the many times they were in captivity because of their disobedience in following His commands.

"You will seek me and find me when you seek me with all of your heart. I will be found by you," declares the Lord, "and will bring you back from captivity."

(Jeremiah 29:13–14)

In my life I have found these verses to be true. God is real and He is easily found when someone has a true desire to seek Him. God knows exactly what is in our heart at every moment. I believe He understands when someone has doubts as they seek the truth. He just desires a sincere heart that wants to know the truth. I have also realized that Jesus was constantly seeking me before I finally accepted Him. The reality is I did not really discover Christ. He pursued me and I finally was receptive to His calling. I also am confident that He is pursuing you and the fact that you are reading this book is no accident.

Other people I have met are not necessarily ignoring Jesus Christ intentionally. They are not making a deliberate attempt to ignore Christianity and do not necessarily have a negative attitude toward Christianity. It is just they are so busy with their life they are not prioritizing any time to pursue the truth. They may even have the good intentions of pursuing the truth "one day" or "when I have more time."

Life today can be extremely hectic. Sometimes it seems we are pulled in so many directions trying to juggle all of the things we feel we need to be doing. Jesus warned us to be careful about being so busy.

> The one who received the seed that fell among the thorns is the one who hears the word, but the worries of this life and the deceitfulness of wealth choke it, making it unfruitful.
>
> (Matthew 13:22)

Notice what Jesus specifically mentioned. He said the worries of this life and the deceitfulness of wealth can choke out God's word to us. If we are honest, many times, the worries of our life are centered on money. It is amazing that we live in a time where we have so many conveniences yet we are stressed so much of the time. We have so many monthly bills that our parents never had. Some of these new bills each month are cable television, cell phones, and internet connections. The problem is every time we add something new, we must pay for it and the financial strain becomes heavier.

Parents many times are kept extremely busy because their kids are involved in a lot of activities as they attempt to excel in school and extracurricular activities. It can be quite a juggling act to get all of the kids where they need to be. Other people are so busy with their careers that they have little time left over for their families or God.

The sad reality is some people have not left any room

for God because of their busy schedules. The result is they are ignoring God even though they are not doing it on purpose. The impact is exactly the same as someone who is intentionally ignoring God.

In the book of Hebrews we are warned to not ignore the salvation offered by Jesus Christ.

> We must pay more careful attention, therefore, to what we have heard, so that we do not drift away. For if the message, spoken by angels, was binding, and every violation and disobedience received its just punishment, how shall we escape if we ignore such a great salvation? This salvation, which was first announced by the Lord, was confirmed to us by those who heard him. God also testified to it by signs, wonders, and various miracles, and gifts of the Holy Spirit distributed according to his will.
>
> (Hebrews 2:1–4)

This passage of scripture asks a very sobering question: *"how shall we escape if we ignore such a great salvation?"* The escape is from God's judgment of our sins. The answer to the question is there is no escape if we ignore the salvation offered by Jesus Christ. Notice the remainder of those verses. It talks about the salvation first being announced by the Lord himself. It then talks about God testifying about the salvation through signs, wonders, miracles, and gifts of the Holy Spirit. Hopefully, those words generate some curiosity in you to pursue what those specific things are and why they are so important.

Have you ever read the Bible? I have heard the Bible

described as God's love letter to man. It has also been called the instruction manual for man. It is such a shame the book God wrote specifically for man, His greatest creation, is ignored by so many people. The Bible teaches us about God and who He really is. It tells what God loves and what God hates. The Bible reveals to us how God's plan from the beginning of creation was for Jesus to be the Savior for all men.

One of the favorite phrases of Jesus when He was speaking was "I tell you the truth." Jesus used this phrase seventy-eight times when He was speaking in the Bible. I think Jesus may have continually used that phrase because He wanted to make sure that we understood that He knew the truth about the things of God and He always spoke the truth. Wouldn't it be worth the time to read the book written by the one and only true God and to seek His truth?

If you are someone who up to this point in your life has either intentionally or unintentionally tuned out anything to do with Christianity and Christ, I trust you realize it is time for you to settle the issue of who Jesus Christ is. The last chapter will give some ways you can start to seek Him.

HYPOCRITICAL CHRISTIANS

Several years ago there was a popular television commercial for a fast food restaurant where a lady would ask the question: "Where's the beef?" She was referring to the competition's hamburgers and implying that there was a lack of beef in their hamburgers.

Unfortunately, I am afraid many people are looking at professing Christians and asking: "Where is the proof that Christ is making a difference in your life?" They see Christians who lie, cheat, and are self-centered. They hear about Christian churches which split or seem to spend half of their time arguing. All of these negative examples reinforce the belief in many people's minds that there is no real value in Christianity and that Christians are "just a bunch of hypocrites." The sad reality is the hypocritical actions of Christians result in making it more difficult for many people to be reached for Christ.

Someone who is not a Christian may not know much about Christianity but the one thing they do know is that Christians are supposed to be good, positive, compassionate, forgiving, and honest people. They are exactly correct. Jesus gave very clear instructions about how His believers are to conduct themselves:

> Simply let your "Yes" be "Yes", and your "No", "No"; anything beyond this comes from the evil one.
>
> (Matthew 5:37)

> Do not judge, and you will not be judged. Do not condemn, and you will not be condemned. Forgive, and you will be forgiven.
>
> (Luke 6:37)

> "You have heard that it was said, 'Love your neighbor and hate your enemies.' But I tell you: Love your enemies and pray for those who persecute you, that you may be sons of your Father in heaven.
>
> (Matthew 5:43–44)

Jesus gave many more instructions about Christian behavior and they are all very admirable qualities. He desires for His believers to live holy lives because He knows the powerful impact it can have on other people being receptive to His message of forgiveness and salvation. Also, when someone strives to be obedient to Christ, the result is they will begin to experience God in a very personal way. Christians are told very clearly in the Bible that their obedience in terms of their actions is what is important.

> Do not merely listen to the word, and so deceive yourselves. Do what it says.
>
> (James 1:22)

Regrettably, if someone desires to find examples of "bad Christians" to prove to themselves that there is no truth or value in Christianity, then they probably have the easiest job in the world. You will not have to look very long or hard to find Christians whose actions are contrary to Jesus' instructions.

Soon after becoming a Christian I read something from the Bible that upset and concerned me greatly. Paul was one of the greatest Christians who ever lived. However, before he accepted Christ, he was one of the chief opponents of Christianity. Paul was the type of person who was very passionate in his beliefs. Before accepting Christ he truly believed Christianity was a false teaching and not in God's will. He did everything in his power to stop the Christian movement.

While on the way to a town called Damascus, Paul encountered Jesus in a powerful way and he realized he had been wrong about Jesus and he was led to become a Christian. Upon accepting Christ, he became just as passionate about spreading the good news of Jesus Christ, he helped lead many people to Christ, and he was used by God to write many of the books in the New Testament.

Another one of the great Christians to ever live was Barnabas. He was also a dedicated Christian, a very humble man, and he loved to encourage people. He was the type of person who could always see the good in a person as opposed to the bad. I think Barnabas looked at people from God's perspective of love and he could see the potential a person had if they focused on God's will for their life. As a matter of fact, when Paul became a Christian, Barnabas was the one to help Paul become accepted by other Christians. Obviously, they were a little wary of Paul, thinking he may be disguising himself to be a Christian as a way to find out more about them in order to continue his persecution.

> When he came to Jerusalem he tried to join the disciples, but they were all afraid of him, not believing he really was a disciple. But Barnabas took him and brought him to the apostles. He told them how Saul on his journey had seen the Lord and that the Lord had spoken to him and how in Damascus he had preached fearlessly in the name of Jesus. So Saul stayed with them and moved about freely in Jerusalem, speaking boldly in the name of the Lord.

> (Acts 9:26–28)

Those verses refer to Paul as Saul. Before becoming a Christian, Paul was known as Saul. However, after his conversion he was known as Paul.

A short time later Paul and Barnabas went on a missionary journey. They went to several cities and they shared the good news of salvation through Jesus Christ. They helped to start new churches. After they completed the first missionary journey they decided to go on a second missionary journey. Barnabas wanted to take along Mark on this journey. Paul objected because Mark had not finished the first journey with them. Mark started out on the first journey, but when the going got tough he returned home.

Knowing the two men, it is easy to see why Paul and Barnabas reacted as they did. I can see Barnabas encouraging Mark to try again. He probably assured him that he would make it this time because it was Barnabas's nature to not give up on someone but to keep lifting them up whenever they needed it. Paul on the other hand was a passionate person who once the mission was set had no intention of backing down. Paul's passion was so important in spreading Christianity in the beginning, and Christians today owe much to Paul's commitment. Paul probably could not relate to someone who was not completely sold out on following his or her beliefs no matter the cost.

> Barnabas wanted to take John, also called Mark with them, but Paul did not think it wise to take him, because he had deserted them in Pamphylia and had not continued with them in the work. They had such a sharp disagreement that they parted company.
>
> (Acts 15:37–39)

I will never forget the moment when I read the words, "sharp disagreement." Immediately, it popped into my mind how could this be. Here are two of the most devoted and dedicated Christians who ever lived and they were arguing. As a young Christian I thought things were going to be smooth sailing inside the church. After all, we were Christians, and even though I knew

I had a lot to learn, I was certain that Christ wanted Christians to get along. This incident let me know early on that Christians are forgiven sinners, but sin is still something that has to be reckoned with and dealt with even after becoming a Christian. Our old nature and self are still there and Christ will begin to change us to become more like Him, but it is usually a slow process for many Christians because it is hard for them to let go of their selfish desires and trust Christ completely.

The good news is even though Paul and Barnabas split up, they still went on their own missionary journeys. Paul went with a man named Silas and Barnabas went with Mark. God took a mess and now twice the work was going to be accomplished. The reality is neither man stopped serving Christ even though he had a dispute with a fellow Christian. It is so sad to see some Christians after having a bad experience in church or with another Christian deciding to just give up. They quit attending church and show no further desire to serve Jesus.

Near the end of Paul's life he was writing to Timothy, a young man who was like a son to Paul.

> Only Luke is with me. Get Mark and bring him with you, because he is helpful to me in my ministry.
>
> (2 Timothy 4:11)

Isn't it great that Barnabas did not give up on Mark and kept encouraging him? Obviously, Mark went on to become an effective Christian and Paul realized that. I think Paul probably learned some important lessons because of his experiences with Mark and Barnabas. Christians will make wrong decisions and will sin but

God does not give up on them and neither should fellow Christians. Also, more mature Christians must realize that newer Christians need encouragement, patience, instruction, and loving correction as they continue their Christian walk.

One of the reasons the Bible is believable to me is because it is so real. There are many people throughout the Bible who had incredible relationships with God yet they sinned. King David immediately pops to mind. Of course, he is famous for slaying Goliath with his slingshot as a boy. He went on to become King and he enjoyed a close relationship with God. However, King David committed adultery and then maneuvered to have the woman's husband put on the front line of battle so that he would be killed. Incredibly, he committed adultery and murder.

It is interesting how God confronted David with his sin. He sent Nathan, a prophet, to tell David a story about a rich man and a poor man.

The Lord sent Nathan to David. When he came to him, he said, "There were two men in a certain town, one rich and the other poor. The rich man had a very large number of sheep and cattle, but the poor man had nothing except one little ewe lamb he had bought. He raised it, and it grew up with him and his children. It shared his food, drank from his cup and even slept in his arms. It was like a daughter to him. Now a traveler came to the rich man, but the rich man refrained from taking one of his own sheep or cattle to prepare a meal for the traveler who had come to him. Instead, he took the ewe lamb that belonged to the poor man and prepared it for the one who had come to him." David burned with anger against the man and said to Nathan, "As surely as the Lord lives, the man who did this deserves to die. He must pay for that lamb four times over, because he did such a thing and had no pity." Then Nathan said to David, "You are the man!"

(2 Samuel 12:1–7)

David is described in the Bible in Acts 13:22 by God as *"a man after my own heart."* Yet he committed great sins and somehow he did not seem to grasp how great they were until God confronted him. It is always amazing how we are able to see other people's sins clearly while minimizing our own. David then confessed his sins to God and was truly repentant for them.

Does the fact that a great man of God did such terrible things make God not real or any less holy? The answer is no. The really great thing about the one and only Holy God is He forgave and restored David even though David did not deserve forgiveness or mercy.

There is much evidence of Christians not living victoriously and in a way that Christ would not approve. Please realize Christians are still human and in many cases have so much growing and developing that needs to take place to become a mature Christian. The phrase "born again" is used many times when someone accepts Christ. I think the phrase is so appropriate. It signifies that a person is starting a new life and is really a baby again in terms of having so much to learn from Christ.

Also, please keep in mind that quite frankly some

people who profess to be Christians may not be. Notice what Jesus says in the following verse.

> Not everyone who says to me, "Lord, Lord" will enter the kingdom of heaven, but only he who does the will of my Father who is in heaven.
>
> (Matthew 7:21)

People go to church sometimes for all of the wrong reasons. I once heard a man say that his business encouraged their employees who were in sales to attend church and to join various civic organizations because it was good for them to be seen there.

Unfortunately, I am afraid some people grew up in church and they consider themselves Christians just because they have always gone to church. They walked "the aisle" and were baptized. The reality is they have never had the life changing experience of admitting they were a sinner and wholeheartedly committing their life to Jesus Christ their Savior. Jesus encountered many "religious" people during His ministry on this Earth and he pointed out they had a heart issue.

> He replied, "Isaiah was right when he prophesied about you hypocrites; as it is written: 'These people honor me with their lips, but their hearts are far from me. They worship me in vain; their teachings are but rules taught by men.' You have let go of the commands of God and are holding on to the traditions of men."
>
> (Mark 7:6–8)

Don't let someone else's experience and example as a Christian, determine whether Christ is real or not for you. In other words, don't write off Christ because of Christians who sin. I beg you to give Christ a chance. He died on the cross for you so that you can have eternal life in Heaven and also so that your life on Earth will be more fulfilling.

I do not want to close this chapter without offering some praise for today's Christians. While it is easy to spot Christians who fail, there are also many Christians who are walking closely with Christ. I guess it is human nature to dwell on the negative instead of the positive. Think about the nightly news and how many positive stories you see versus the number of negative stories. When a parent looks at a report card, how much focus does the worst grade get in relation to the best grade? There is a great deal of good that takes place in churches. Sunday School classes helping serve meals at the local rescue mission, church members checking on senior citizens during inclement weather, and church members being there for one another when tragedies strike. Unfortunately, bad news travels faster and seems to cause much more excitement than good news. Also, some people want to see the bad things that Christians do so that they can continue to satisfy their belief that Christianity has no value.

In conclusion, if you are one of the people who have written off Christ because of the failures of Christians, I hope something you read in this chapter will cause you to step back and reconsider. I would simply encourage you to take your focus off of Christians and turn your attention to Christ. The last chapter will offer some practical steps on how to focus on Christ.

It Is All About the Money

Money is a very touchy issue for many people when they think about religion. People are very suspicious about religious leaders and their motivation when it comes to dealing with money. Unfortunately, there have been examples of religious leaders being corrupt in the area of money and it is little wonder why people are suspicious. Some people have used these examples to conclude that the primary focus of religion is getting money from people.

Corruption in the area of money and religion has been around from the beginning. Judas was one of the twelve disciples of Jesus. Judas was also the treasurer for the disciples. Once when a young woman named Mary used expensive perfume to wipe Jesus' feet, Judas objected saying that the perfume could have been sold and the money given to the poor. What was Judas's real motivation?

> He did not say this because he cared about the poor but because he was a thief; as keeper of the money bag, he used to help himself to what was put into it.
>
> (John 12:6)

Sadly, money corrupts and truly is the motivation behind a great deal of evil. Religion is not excluded from the corruption caused by the love of money. Judas witnessed incredible miracles performed by Jesus. He saw Jesus raise people from the dead, give sight to the blind, make the lame walk, and many other amazing miracles. He sat at the feet of Jesus and heard Jesus teach about God and the things that truly mattered to God. Even after witnessing all of these miracles and the power of God first hand, Judas still sold Jesus out for money. Judas disclosed the location of Jesus to those opposing Jesus so they could arrest and crucify Him. The love of money is indeed a powerful force.

What does God expect from us in terms of money? In the book of Leviticus, God gives instructions on what He expects from us.

> A tithe of everything from the land, whether the grain from the soil or fruit from the trees, belongs to the Lord, it is holy to the Lord.
>
> (Leviticus 27:30)

A tithe is ten percent. God expects us to give back ten percent of our earnings to Him. Why? Because it honors Him and is a demonstration that we love Him. God provides life and all of our blessings; by giving back to Him we are worshiping Him and acknowledging He has blessed us.

God is our creator. Since He created us, He knows everything there is to know about us. He knows what makes us tick and He also knows we were created to worship. He desires for us to worship Him because He knows that is what is best for us. He wants us to make Him the priority of our life because He loves us and He will lead us in the right direction. He desires what is best for our lives. He knows what will give us true joy and peace. He wants to guide us and protect us.

Even there your hand will guide me, your right hand will hold me fast.

(Psalm 139:10)

David wrote that particular verse in Psalm. David realized how much God cared for him and how he needed to let God guide him. David also realized that God was always concerned about him and he was secure in God's hand.

God knows money can easily become the focus of our lives and something we worship. God knows that if our number one priority is money, we will never be satisfied. No matter how much money we have we will always want a little more.

Whoever loves money never has money enough;

whoever loves wealth is never satisfied with his income. This too is meaningless.

(Ecclesiastes 5:10)

Just like drugs, money can become very destructive to us if we allow ourselves to become addicted to it. God wants us to put our trust in Him. The Bible tells us in several places that God is a jealous God. He is jealous when we put something ahead of Him. He created us in order to have a relationship with us and He loves us. One of the Ten Commandments makes it very clear that we should never worship anything but Him.

You shall not make for yourself an idol in the form of anything in heaven above or on the earth beneath or in the waters below. You shall not bow down to them or worship them; for I, the Lord your God, am a jealous God...

(Exodus 20:4–5)

Money can easily become the idol of someone's life. Once a certain rich ruler came to Jesus and wanted to know what he must do to inherit eternal life. Jesus told him he must keep the commandments. The man indicated that he had kept all of the commandments since he was a boy. Jesus then told him one more thing that he must do.

When Jesus heard this, he said to him, "You still lack one thing. Sell everything you have and give to the poor, and you will have treasure in heaven. Then come, follow me."

(Luke 18:22)

When the rich ruler heard this he became sad and left because the Bible tells us that he was a man of great wealth. Why did Jesus make such a huge request of this man? Is Jesus saying that we can't have a lot of money? What happened to the tithe or ten percent requirement? Jesus knows our hearts and He knew this man's heart. Jesus knew that the priority in this man's life was his money. As long as he had a lot of money then money was always going to be his primary focus and the god of his life. In order for Jesus to be the primary focus for this man, the money needed to go. In other words, he had to get rid of his idol so that Jesus could become the center of his life.

Another problem with money is the false security it brings. We can fall into the trap of thinking that if I have a lot of money then everything is okay in my life. Jesus told a parable of a man who thought that same way.

And he told them this parable: "The ground of a certain rich man produced a good crop. He thought to himself, 'What shall I do? I have no place to store my crops.' Then he said, 'This is what I'll do. I will tear down my barns and build bigger ones, and there I will store all my grain and my goods. And I'll say to myself, "You have plenty of good things laid up for many years. Take life easy; eat, drink, and be merry."

' But God said to him, 'You fool! This very night your life will be demanded from you. Then who will get what you have prepared for yourself.' This is how it will be with anyone who stores up things for himself but is not rich toward God."

(Luke 12:16–21)

Jesus was pointing out that the money was not going to be any further benefit to the rich man because he was going to die that night. Obviously, his money would simply be passed on to someone else. What would be beneficial to the man as he faced death is whether he was rich toward God or not. Being rich toward God has nothing to do with how much money we have. It does involve how we use our money and the importance we place on it. Jesus pointed out this truth once to His disciples as He witnessed people giving their offering to the church.

Jesus sat down opposite the place where the offerings were put and watched the crowd putting their money into the temple treasury. Many rich people threw in large amounts. But a poor widow came and put in two very small copper coins, worth only a fraction of a penny. Calling his disciples to him, Jesus said, "I tell you the truth, this poor widow has put more into the treasury than all the others. They all gave out of their wealth; but she, out of her poverty, put in everything—all she had to live on."

(Mark 12:41–44)

The poor widow was rich toward God. From a strictly human standpoint it made absolutely no sense for her to put the money in the offering. She needed it just for the basic necessities of life. However, she realized that her most basic and important need was having the right relationship with God. Giving her offering was something she wanted to do in order to show her love and dependence on her Heavenly Father. She was indeed "rich toward God" and she obviously believed in the truth of Psalm 139:10 that David wrote.

Besides the security that money seems to offer, there are other appealing aspects that can cause us to fall under its influence. Money brings prestige. When someone has a lot of money other people will honor them and show them a lot of respect. It makes them feel special and proud. I think deep down they know that many people are really treating them special because of the money they have and not because of the person they really are. Therefore, money becomes even more important to them because they do not want to lose their identity and the respect that the money brings them.

Money can be a very good thing. It can be used to help so many people. The problem is when we allow it to become the main thing in our life. When Jesus selected the twelve disciples He began to teach them things they needed to know about God. One of the most important lessons He taught them was where they needed to put their trust. Once He sent the twelve disciples out to preach with the message that people should repent and turn to God. He also gave the disciples the power to perform healing of people who were sick or possessed by evil spirits. Notice the instructions He gave them as they left.

These were his instructions: "Take nothing for the journey except a staff—no bread, no bag, no money in your belts."

(Mark 6:8)

Why would Jesus give them those instructions? Shouldn't we plan and be prepared? Jesus was teaching them they could indeed trust God to provide for their needs when they were being obedient to Him. It is one thing to say we trust God to take care of us but the real test is when we actually demonstrate it. Jesus wanted them to actually experience what it meant to trust God completely. Ultimately, Jesus wants us to know that we can also trust God and He is the only one that can be trusted completely.

I have a good friend who has a great testimony about how he originally felt about church and money. He finally agreed to attend church with his wife but he let her know that if the pastor started talking about money then he was out of there. After attending church for a while, he realized his need to be forgiven for his sins and he accepted Christ and joined the church. Shortly after this the pastor did preach a sermon on tithing. It did not matter to him then, giving to God and the church was not something he resented or felt suspicious about anymore. Giving was something he wanted to do now. Eventually my friend agreed to serve on the Finance Committee of the church. God does have a sense of humor.

Are your suspicions about religion and money keeping you from being open to the message of salvation through Jesus Christ? Just because Judas was evil in the area of money does not diminish who Jesus is, and just because there are still examples of corruption today does not diminish who Jesus is. The reality is the vast majority of churches and religious organizations are very good stewards of their money.

It is amazing when you think about all of the planes flying every day. When there is a plane crash it is rightfully given a lot of media coverage and is a great tragedy. However, it does not eliminate the fact that there are thousands of safe flights taking place every week. Likewise, when there is an example of a religious organization or leader being corrupt in the area of money, it does not change the fact that most religious organizations and leaders are handling their money correctly and accomplishing a lot of good with their money.

The Bible is very clear about the type of giver that pleases God.

Each man should give what he has decided in his heart to give, not reluctantly or under compulsion, for God loves a cheerful giver.

(2 Corinthians 9:7)

My hope is that you will decide that you are going to pursue the truth about who Jesus is and not let money be a stumbling block any longer. The truth is Jesus loves you and not your money. Admit to God that you have doubts especially in the area of money but you really do want to know the truth about Jesus. If you are sincere, God will honor your request and someday you will find yourself being a cheerful giver.

My Sins are Too Great

Some people may think that God could never forgive or love them because of the terrible things they have done. Jesus makes it very clear who He came to Earth for:

> On hearing this, Jesus said to them, "It is not the healthy who need a doctor, but the sick. I have not come to call the righteous, but sinners."
>
> (Mark 2:17)

Jesus made the above statement right after the Jewish religious leaders questioned why Jesus was eating with "sinners". These religious leaders felt they were superior to most people when in reality they displeased Jesus greatly because of their self-righteousness. Jesus came to Earth and died on the cross so that people could be cleansed from their sins because He provided a perfect sacrifice for our sins. If you say that God could never forgive you or want you in Heaven, then you are really saying that your sins are greater than God's forgiveness. God's grace is bigger than all of your sins plus the sins of the entire world.

> My dear children, I write this to you so that you will not sin. But if anybody does sin, we have one who speaks to the Father in our defense—Jesus Christ, the Righteous One. He is the atoning sacrifice for our sins, and not only for ours but also for the sins of the whole world.
>
> (1 John 2:1–2)

There are many examples from the Bible to show how Christ wants you to turn to Him no matter how many sins you have committed. One such example deals with the prodigal son. A father had two sons. The younger son came to the father one day and told his father he wanted his share of the inheritance because he was leaving. The father gave the son what he requested.

> "Not long after that, the younger son got together all he had, set off for a distant country and there squandered his wealth in wild living. After he had spent everything, there was a severe famine in that whole country, and he began to be in need. So, he went and

hired himself out to a citizen of that country, who sent him to his fields to feed pigs. He longed to fill his stomach with the pods that the pigs were eating, but no one gave him anything."

(Luke 15:13–16)

The situation became so desperate the son decided to return to his father and confess his sins and hoped that maybe his father would hire him to be a servant. He figured that his sins and the dishonor he had brought on his family meant he did not deserve to be treated like a son anymore by his father. He probably could not imagine that his father would ever want to claim him as a son because of how foolishly he had acted. Notice the father's reaction when he saw his son approaching their home.

"So he got up and went to his Father. But while he was still a long way off, his father saw him and was filled with compassion for him: he ran to his son, threw his arms around him and kissed him. The son said to him, 'Father, I have sinned against heaven and against you. I am no longer worthy to be called your son.'"

(Luke 15:20–21)

One of the many great things about this parable is the father ran and welcomed the son without knowing that the son was coming home to say he was sorry. It could have been that the son was coming home to request more money. The reason did not matter to the father. He was just so happy to see his son, and notice it emphasized he was filled with compassion for him. However, it is important to note the confession that the son made. The son was genuinely sorry for his behavior and really hoped his father was not going to turn him away.

The son probably could have never imagined such a warm welcome from his father who had a feast to celebrate the return of his son. The son did not deserve the welcome or the party. The key was his father loved him unconditionally and had compassion for him. If you think your sins are too great and you do not deserve forgiveness, you are exactly right about not deserving forgiveness. The good news is God's mercy, compassion, and unconditional love results in Him giving us forgiveness. We just have to turn to Him, confess our sins, and confess our need for Jesus Christ as our Savior.

Paul's life is another example of how God can forgive and change someone's life regardless of the sins they have committed. As was mentioned in chapter two, Paul originally thought Christianity was a false teaching and he did everything in his power to stop it from spreading. He condoned the killing of the first Christian martyr, Stephen. Notice how passionate Paul was in his efforts to persecute the Christian believers.

> But Saul began to destroy the church. Going from house to house, he dragged off men and women and put them in prison.
>
> (Acts 8:3)

(Note: Please remember Paul was known as Saul before he became a Christian.)

It would seem if there was anyone who God would

not love or want to forgive it would be Paul. After all, he was doing everything in his power to destroy God's plan of salvation for all men. He was opposing God directly. Instead of condemning Paul and giving up on him, God pursued Paul so that he would understand the truth about Jesus.

> Meanwhile, Saul was still breathing out murderous threats against the Lord's disciples. He went to the high priest and asked him for letters to the synagogues in Damascus, so that if he found any there who belonged to the Way, whether men or women, he might take them as prisoners to Jerusalem. As he neared Damascus on his journey, suddenly a light from heaven flashed around him. He fell to the ground and heard a voice say to him, "Saul, Saul, why do you persecute me?" "Who are you, Lord?" Saul asked. "I am Jesus, whom you are persecuting," he replied. "Now get up and go into the city, and you will be told what you must do."
>
> (Acts 9:1–6)

Paul was actually blinded for three days because of this experience. Can you imagine the emotions he must have felt during those three days? He realized how wrong he had been about Jesus. He probably remembered all of the things he had done to the Christians. He may have wondered if he would ever see again and what was God going to do to him. Paul was changed for life and he accepted Jesus as his Savior. He totally committed the rest of his life to serving Jesus and is truly an example of someone whose purpose in life was to be obedient to Jesus.

Paul was extremely grateful to God for saving him and showing him the truth. He realized how wrong he had been about Jesus and how ignorant he had been as he indicated in the book of First Timothy. Notice Paul also considered himself to be the worst of sinners.

I thank Christ Jesus our Lord, who has given me strength, that he considered me faithful, appointing me to his service. Even though I was once a blasphemer and a persecutor and a violent man, I was shown mercy because I acted in ignorance and unbelief. The grace of our Lord was poured out on me abundantly, along with the faith and love that are in Christ Jesus. Here is a trustworthy saying that deserves full acceptance: Christ Jesus came into the world to save sinners–of whom I am the worst. But for that very reason I was shown mercy so that in me, the worst of sinners, Christ Jesus might display his unlimited patience as an example for those who would believe on him and receive eternal life.

(I Timothy 1:12–16)

God still seeks us out and wants us to turn to Him and accept His forgiveness just as Paul did. If you have been thinking there is no hope for you and you do not deserve forgiveness, please reconsider. Christ died on the cross for you just as much as He did for every other person. Know how important you are to Him, and do not make His sacrifice on the cross be in vain as far as you are concerned. God has a purpose for your life just like He did for Paul.

Jesus came for every single person because every person is a sinner and needs forgiveness. Jesus illustrated this fact one day when a woman was brought to Him who had been caught committing adultery. The people who brought the woman were the self-righteous teachers of the law who were constantly trying to trap Jesus into doing something against the Jewish law so they would have something to arrest Him for. The Jewish law said the woman should be stoned and they wanted to know what Jesus thought should be done to the woman. Notice what Jesus did and how He responded.

> They were using this question as a trap, in order to have a basis for accusing him. But Jesus bent down and started to write on the ground with his finger. When they kept on questioning him, he straightened up and said to them, "If any one of you is without sin, let him be the first to throw a stone at her." Again he stooped down and wrote on the ground. At this, those who heard began to go away one at a time, the older ones first, until only Jesus was left, with the woman still standing there. Jesus straightened up and asked her, "Woman, where are they? Has no one condemned you? "No one, sir," she said. "Then neither do I condemn you," Jesus declared, "Go now and leave your life of sin."
>
> (John 8:6–11)

The Bible does not tell us what Jesus was writing on the ground. Was He just doodling? I doubt it. Some people have speculated that Jesus was writing down some of the sins of the people who had brought the woman to Him. Some of them may have had some "secret" sins in their life and Jesus was listing them. What we do know for sure is every person left because they knew that they were not without sin in their lives and that was the point Jesus wanted them to realize.

We love to categorize sins in terms of their seriousness. It is true that some sins are more serious than others in terms of their human impact. For example, I would much rather that you lie to me than kill me. However, in the eyes of God both are sins and result in the need for confession so that forgiveness can be granted. Notice what Jesus said about who God wants to have eternal life.

> "For my Father's will is that everyone who looks to the Son and believes in him shall have eternal life, and I will raise him up at the last day."
>
> (John 6:40)

> The Lord is not slow in keeping his promise, as some understand slowness. He is patient with you, not wanting anyone to perish, but everyone to come to repentance.
>
> (2 Peter 3:9)

Notice that Jesus did not put any type of qualifications on who God wants to see in Heaven other than belief in Jesus. There were no stipulations about how many sins someone commits or about how serious someone's sins are. God's desire and will is for every person to accept Jesus Christ because He does not want "anyone to perish."

The Bible tells us very clearly that we cannot work our way into Heaven. Our ability to go to Heaven is based solely on our accepting Jesus Christ in faith.

> For it is by grace you have been saved, through faith–and this is not from yourselves, it is the gift of God–not by works, so that no one can boast.
>
> (Ephesians 2:8–9)

If the number of our sins or the seriousness of our sins could exclude us from the salvation of Jesus Christ, then that is in effect saying that our "works" do have a bearing on our salvation. In this case, it would not be positive works to earn salvation but it would be negative works that would forfeit our right to salvation. The truth according to the Bible is that our works do not determine our salvation. We just have to believe in Jesus. This fact may sound too easy, but if our works had any bearing on our salvation, then God knows that pride and boasting would become an issue. In other words, people would be feeling a sense of accomplishment in being able to go to Heaven. Their focus would be on themselves and not on God.

Quite frankly, if you are feeling a lot of guilt about your sins then that is actually a good sign. You realize the seriousness of sin and you would love for that nagging guilt to be removed. The only solution is to turn to God for His forgiveness. Notice how far the following verses indicate our sins are from us if we will just accept God's forgiveness and His plan of salvation.

For as high as the heavens are above the earth, so great is his love for those who fear him; as far as the east is from the west, so far has he removed our transgressions from us. As a father has compassion on his children, so the Lord has compassion on those who fear him;

(Psalm 103:11–13)

King David, when confronted by the prophet Nathan with his sins of adultery and murder, acknowledged why sin is so bad.

Then David said to Nathan, "I have sinned against the Lord."

(2 Samuel 12:13)

Our sins are against a Holy God. Fortunately, our Holy God loves us and wants to forgive us no matter what we have done. He wants everyone to be saved and everyone definitely includes you. Therefore, shift your attention off of your sins and focus on Jesus Christ who is the only one that can provide the forgiveness and peace that you are seeking.

It is Too Late for Me

Perhaps you are an adult and maybe even a senior citizen who believes it is too late for you to become a Christian. You may feel that it is ridiculous to even think about any changes in your life now. The really good news is that it is not too late. God wants very much for you to accept Him now.

Jesus gave a great example in the Bible to highlight that God is offering us salvation and hope even when we think it may be too late. There was a landowner who needed workers for his vineyard. He went out at six in the morning and hired some men to work and he agreed to pay them a denarius which would have been a fair wage for day's worth of work. At nine o'clock he went out and found some more men looking for work and hired them. For this second group of workers he simply said he would pay them what was right and he did not set a specific figure with them like he did for the first group. The workers would have done this because anything would be better than nothing. Also, many people lived day to day, and with no work and no money for a particular day meant there would be no food for that day. He did the exact same thing at noon, three o'clock, and five o'clock. At the end of the day when it came time to pay the workers, the landowner started with the workers that he hired last. He paid them a denarius. He also paid the workers he hired first a denarius.

Obviously, the workers hired first were not happy and thought they had been cheated and treated unfairly. The landowner responded to the unhappy workers.

> But he answered one of them, "Friend I am not being unfair to you. Didn't you agree to work for a denarius? Take your pay and go. I want to give the man who was hired last the same as I gave you. Don't I have the right to do what I want with my own money? Or are you envious because I am generous?"
>
> (Matthew 20:13–15)

I think Jesus' message in this story is it is never too late as long as we are willing to accept His forgiveness. It is God's right to offer His mercy and forgiveness whenever and to whomever He desires. Remember, eternity is a very long time. It is forever and ever while our time on this Earth is an extremely short time when compared to eternity. Do you think God would ever deny someone the opportunity to accept the gift of salvation and spend eternity in Heaven just because they did not accept Him in the first fifty, sixty, or even 100 years of their life? God just wants us to accept His forgiveness and grace. Therefore, please do not let your age be an obstacle as you consider Jesus Christ.

One might argue then, "I will just wait until I am old and then I will check out Jesus Christ and His promises." I see two major problems with that reasoning.

A lot of people will die today that had no idea when they woke up this morning that today would be their last day on Earth. Nobody can be certain that they will live another day. Recently, two people I knew who were young died suddenly in tragic accidents. I am sure both of them did not expect that day to be their last one when they went to work that morning. Fortunately, both of these men were Christians and while their sudden death was so sad and their families and friends miss them tremendously, it is comforting to know they are in Heaven. Therefore, no one can be assured they will live to an old age.

The big problem with saying I will delay my decision is I am afraid you are thinking it is better to live this life without Christ than to live it with Him. Even though I am spending a lot of time in this book talking about your eternal future and the need to know Jesus Christ in order to get to Heaven, please realize there is tremendous value in accepting Christ immediately so that He can be a part of your day to day existence on this Earth.

Think back to the story of the landowner and the workers. Even though the workers hired first thought they were being treated unfairly, they did not think about the advantage they had that day over the workers hired last. Recall that the workers in those days lived day to day, and if they did not get paid for a day it usually meant they were not going to have food for that particular day. The workers hired first had the knowledge and assurance that food would be available for them all day long. Can you imagine the anxiety the workers hired at five o'clock were experiencing? They maybe were even feeling guilty because they had not been out in the marketplace first thing in the morning like the workers hired at six o'clock were. They probably felt like it was too late for them now and there was no hope of food for that day.

Christ did not just come and die on the cross so you can spend eternity in Heaven. He came to comfort, encourage, instruct, and reassure you to help you get through each day. He does not want each day for us to be a matter of just trying to survive and hang on. Instead His desire is for our life to be one that could be described as thriving. Christ tells us He came to provide an abundant life.

> I am come that they might have life and that they might have it more abundantly.
>
> (John 10:10 KJV)

Chapter 9 will focus in more detail on some of the advantages and benefits of having a relationship with Christ in this life.

If you are near the end of your life and you are approaching your five o'clock hour, please know it is not too late to accept Christ. While it is unfortunate that you did not accept Him earlier and have the joy of living each day with the knowledge of His presence and His promise of spending eternity in Heaven, the important thing now is to turn to Him and accept His generous gift of salvation. His desire is for you to spend eternity with Him and it is never too late as long as you are living.

Another great example to show it is never too late to accept Christ while on this Earth is found when Jesus died on the cross. Jesus was crucified at the same time as two thieves. One of the thieves hurled insults at Jesus and mocked Him by saying if Jesus was really Christ then He should save himself. The other thief rebuked the thief who was mocking Jesus.

> But the other criminal rebuked him. "Don't you fear God," he said, "since you are under the same sentence? We are punished justly, for we are getting what our deeds deserve. But this man has done nothing wrong." Then he said, "Jesus, remember me when you come into your kingdom. Jesus answered him, "I tell you the truth, today you will be with me in paradise."
>
> (Luke 23:40–43)

The thief realized he deserved his punishment because he was guilty. He acknowledged his sins and he realized his only hope as he was facing death was Jesus. Jesus provided the forgiveness the man sought.

I have often heard it said it is much harder for a person to accept Christ the older they get. A friend shared with me recently that one of her friends was at a banquet and the speaker reported that once he was at a Christian conference of 2500 men and it was revealed during the conference that eighty-eight percent of the 2500 men accepted Christ before the age of twelve. Why is it more difficult for an adult to accept Christ? I think there are several possible explanations.

When someone experiences success from the world's perspective, they can become prideful and begin to think they do not need Christ because they are doing just fine on their own. Also, an adult tends to rely on reason for everything. The bottom line is the key ingredient to pleasing God and accepting Jesus Christ is having faith in Him and in His promises. Jesus illustrated this fact by talking about children.

> "Let the little children come to me, and do not hinder them, for the kingdom of God belongs to such as these. I tell you the truth, anyone who will not receive the kingdom of God like a little child will never enter it."
>
> (Luke 18:16–17)

Children must have faith. They accept many things their parents tell them because they trust their parents even though some things do not make sense to them. Jesus is letting us know we must have this child-like faith in Him as we accept Him as our Savior. He loves it when we show faith in Him because it shows we love Him and we trust Him.

If you are a parent, one of the best reasons to pursue the truth about Jesus is for the sake of your children. Children do imitate and trust their parents. The beliefs and values instilled into children by their parents will in many cases remain with them for their entire life.

Train a child in the way he should go, and when he is old he will not turn from it.

(Proverbs 22:6)

What are you teaching your children? Don't you want to find out if it is true that Jesus is the only way to Heaven, in order to properly train your child? Children are a precious gift from God and a parent's major responsibilities are to love them and to teach them about God.

Some adults who have maybe been very critical of Christianity and Christians for most of their life may also feel that if they accept Christ they are admitting they were wrong all of their earlier years. Think back to Paul's life. He was the chief opponent of Christianity. Once he realized how wrong he had been about Jesus, he accepted the truth. It may have been hard for him to swallow his pride and admit to himself and others he had been completely wrong about Jesus and Christianity. Pride is a very detrimental trait. Proverbs tells us very clearly the negative impact of pride.

"Pride goes before destruction."

(Proverbs 16:18)

Christ died for your sins and wants you to accept His gift of salvation. If you are an older person just realize the saying "better late than never" is very true when talking about accepting the salvation offered by Jesus. If most of your family or friends are not Christians you may also be concerned about what they will think and how they will react if you become a Christian. It could very well be your friends are another reason Christ wants you to accept Him now. Since it is harder for people to accept Christ the older they are, it may be you are the one God wants to use to help lead your friends to accept Christ as well. There is no greater joy than leading someone to Christ and knowing that their eternal destination is Heaven.

One of the joys of reading the Bible is realizing how great God is and learning about the ways of God. He constantly uses people to do His will in ways which are amazing. He loves to use people's weaknesses in order to accomplish His purposes. I think He does that so people will rely on Him and not on themselves. He once made a promise to Abraham that he would be the father of a great nation. The problem was Abraham's wife had not been able to have a child and now they were well past the age when a couple had children.

> God also said to Abraham, "As for Sarai your wife, you are no longer to call her Sarai; her name will be Sarah. I will bless her and will surely give you a son by her. I will bless her so that she will be the mother of nations; kings of peoples will come from her." Abraham fell facedown; he laughed and said to himself, "Will a son be born to a man a hundred years old? Will Sarah bear a child at the age of ninety?"
>
> (Genesis 17:15–17)

It is easy to understand Abraham's amazement at what God was saying. It just seemed way too late for them to be having children. Sarah also laughed at the thought of her having a child at her age. I love God's response to them.

Then the Lord said to Abraham, "Why did Sarah laugh and say, 'Will I really have a child, now that I am old?' Is anything too hard for the Lord? I will return to you at the appointed time next year and Sarah will have a son."

(Genesis 18:13–14)

Nothing of course is too hard for God. It was very easy for Him to bless Abraham and Sarah with a child if that was His will for them no matter how old they were. Likewise, time has not passed you by as far as the Lord is concerned. He still has a plan for the rest of your life. The question is whether or not you are willing to accept Jesus as your Savior and then let the Lord lead you. Only God knows what He has in store for you, and don't you want to find out?

It is definitely not too late for you. There will be great joy in Heaven if you accept Christ. Please make the decision today that you are not going to let any obstacle associated with age keep you from being open to salvation through Jesus Christ. Please follow the steps outlined in the last chapter and pursue for yourself the truth about Jesus.

WHERE HAS GOD BEEN IN MY LIFE?

L ife has been extremely difficult for a lot of
people. They have faced many difficult situations or experienced a lot of tragedy in their life.
When they look at their circumstances compared to a lot
of people around them, they may wonder why doesn't
God love me or why doesn't He bless me? It is easy for
them to conclude there must not be a God or if He exists
then He is unfair and they want no part of Him.

This chapter was the toughest chapter for me to write.
It was not tough for me because I have doubts about
God's love and concern for every person. It was tough
because I feel I have been very fortunate in my life. I have

a wonderful wife who I admire and love greatly. God has also blessed us with two great sons that have proven to be two of my best friends. I truly enjoy spending time with them and I value my relationship with them. I have great parents who love me unconditionally and continually demonstrate their love for me. My problem in addressing this particular subject was how could I possibly relate to someone who has had a lot of heartache? I wondered if I could address this area without appearing to be insensitive to someone's situation. In other words I wondered if people would say, "It is awfully easy for you to say or believe that."

I went back and forth wondering if I should just leave this chapter out of this book. After wrestling with this dilemma, I finally felt led by God to include this chapter. The bottom line is the only reason I decided to write this book was to hopefully help people overcome whatever was keeping them from considering the message of salvation through Jesus Christ. Since I know a lot of people doubt God and His love for them because of the tough circumstances of their life, I felt it would really be a disservice to them to leave this chapter out because I truly believe the greatest tragedy in life is someone not coming to know Jesus Christ. In other words, I felt I could be hurting someone in the worst way possible by not attempting to address this subject. Jesus Christ is the best news there is and people with a lot of heartache need the good news. If I intentionally left this chapter out would I maybe in effect be saying that perhaps some people had a legitimate argument against God? I feel with all of my heart that God cares deeply for every person.

The obvious question for many people who experience a lot of heartache and tragedy is "Why me?" That is a difficult question and quite honestly it is probably impossible to give a specific answer to a particular person. I would like to share some examples from the Bible of people who suffered and some conclusions we can draw from their particular situations. My hope and prayer is if you are someone who has experienced a great deal of sorrow, you will sense God's love and concern for you as you read this chapter and feel led to truly seek God.

Many times people assume their trouble is caused by sin in their life and they are being disciplined by God. It is true that sin does have consequences and a lot of problems that people have are self-inflicted because of their sin. When David committed his terrible sins of adultery and murder, God did forgive and restore David. However, the sin did result in bringing a lot of heartache to David and one of the consequences was the life of his son.

> But because by doing this you have made the enemies of the Lord show utter contempt, the son born to you will die.
>
> (2 Samuel 12:14)

The Bible also makes it clear that not all trouble is a result of sin. I would like to point out two specific instances where suffering was not a result of sin.

Jesus and His disciples were walking along one day and they came upon a blind man. The disciples questioned Jesus about whose sin caused this man to be blind. They wondered if it was because of the man's sin or was it because of his parents' sin. The disciples felt like many people of that time that this man was blind because he was being punished for his sins or the sins of his family. Notice how Jesus answered their question.

> "Neither this man nor his parents sinned," said Jesus, "but this happened so that the work of God might be displayed in his life."
>
> (John 9:3)

Jesus then proceeded to heal the man. The man, of course, was thrilled and began to tell people who had healed him. The religious leaders questioned the man and he told them exactly how Jesus had healed him. They asked the healed man who he thought Jesus was, and the man at this point said he thought Jesus was a prophet.

The religious leaders were jealous of Jesus and did not like the popularity Jesus was receiving. They kept questioning the man and wanted the man to give the glory to God because they said Jesus was a sinner. The religious leaders indicated Jesus was a sinner because He had healed the man on the Sabbath. The man's response to their accusation was he did not know if Jesus was a sinner or not, but the thing he knew for sure was, *"I was blind but now I see!"* The man would not back down from the truth that it was Jesus who had healed him. The religious leaders finally became so frustrated that they threw him out of their presence.

Jesus heard what had happened and went and found the man. Jesus then asked the man:

> "Do you believe in the Son of Man?"
>
> (John 9:35)

The healed man then asked Jesus who is this Son of Man. He requested that Jesus tell him so that he could believe in Him.

> Jesus said, "You have now seen him; in fact, he is the one speaking with you." Then the man said, "Lord, I believe," and he worshiped him. Jesus said, "For judgment I have come into this world, so that the blind will see and those who see will become blind."
>
> (John 9:37–39)

We are told very plainly by Jesus that this man's physical blindness was not caused by sin. The real miracle in this man's life was not the fact that he was able to finally physically see, but that his heart was opened to the salvation that Jesus provides. I believe with all of my heart that this man will spend forever in Heaven because of his belief in Jesus Christ.

I suppose some may say it was not fair that this man still suffered with being blind for all of those years. Is it possible that if this particular man had been able to physically see he would have ended up being like the religious leaders and been spiritually blind? Or did God allow this man to be born blind because God knew he would react to his healing by being thankful and joyful instead of being bitter for all of the years that he had been blind. I think that man would tell us today those years of being blind were well worth the encounter he had with Jesus and the free gift of grace that Jesus provided to him. Only God knows for sure why this particular man was born blind but what a happy ending.

Another example from the Bible that illustrates tragedy or troubles are not necessarily caused by sin is found in the life of Job. Job was a very wealthy man and he had seven sons and three daughters. Job was also a man who loved God. The Bible tells us that one day Satan came into the presence of God and God questioned Satan about where he had been. Satan responded that he had been roaming the earth. Obviously, he was roaming about doing evil. God then did something rather surprising. He mentioned Job's name:

> Then the Lord said to Satan, "Have you considered my servant Job? There is no one on earth like him; he is blameless and upright, a man who fears God and shuns evil."
>
> (Job 1:8)

First of all, what an awesome compliment God paid Job. Job must have been a special man for God to praise him so highly. The surprising thing is how much God praised Job to Satan. Obviously, the praise would make Satan mad and make him want to cause Job to sin in order to hurt God. Satan then tells God that the only reason Job praises God is because God has blessed him so much. Satan says that if Job lost all that he had then Job would curse God. God then gave Satan permission to attack Job but He told Satan he was not to harm Job physically.

In one day's time all of Job's oxen, donkeys, sheep, and camels were either killed or stolen. During the same day Job also received word that all ten of his children had been killed. How did Job react to such terrible disasters one right after the other?

At this, Job got up and tore his robe and shaved his head. Then he fell to the ground in worship and said: "Naked I came from my mother's womb, and naked I will depart. The Lord gave and the Lord has taken away; may the name of the Lord be praised." In all this, Job did not sin by charging God with wrongdoing.

(Job 1:20–22)

Job obviously was a man of great faith with a deep trust and love for God. Of course, Satan does not give up so easily. He then told God that really what a man cares most for is his own physical well being and that Job would surely curse God if Job was physically harmed. God then gave Satan permission to attack Job's body but Satan was not allowed to kill Job. Satan went out and caused Job to have painful sores from his feet to the top of his head. Job's wife told Job he should curse God. What was Job's reaction to his wife's request?

He replied, "You are talking like a foolish woman. Shall we accept good from God, and not trouble?" In all this, Job did not sin in what he said.

(Job 2:10)

I am sure Satan was absolutely stunned that Job did not curse God because of all the things that had happened to him. If you continue reading the book of Job you will learn that some of Job's friends visited him. They concluded Job's situation was a result of sin in his life and Job needed to confess his sin. Job rejected their conclusion.

Job was not sure why everything had happened to him but he did not think it was because of sin in his life. Job just wanted a chance to talk to God about his situation. He felt that maybe God just did not quite understand his situation and he wanted to fill God in on some things. He desired to have an audience with God.

> But I desire to speak to the Almighty and to argue my case with God.
>
> (Job 13:3)

Eventually Job got his wish. God did speak with Job and He asked Job a lot of questions about the creation of the earth that Job could not possibly answer. He also asked Job some questions to indicate to Job that God was very well aware of everything that was happening and was going to happen on His earth.

> Do you know when the mountain goats give birth? Do you watch when the doe bears her fawn? Do you count the months till they bear? Do you know the time they give birth?
>
> (Job 39:1–2)

God's message to Job was very clear. If God knew exactly when mountain goats give birth to their babies, did Job think God was going to miss something going on in Job's life? God continued to bombard Job with questions that Job had no way of answering. All of the questions caused Job to reflect on who he was and who God is.

Then Job replied to the Lord "I know that you can do all things; no plan of yours can be thwarted. You asked, "Who is this that obscures my counsel without knowledge?" Surely, I spoke of things I did not understand, things too wonderful for me to know.

(Job 42:1–3)

God never did explain to Job why everything happened to him and of His conversation with Satan. Job did not even seem to want to know anymore. After his encounter with God, Job realized God's power and majesty and that was enough for Job. God did restore Job's wealth and Job once again was blessed with seven sons and three daughters.

The question again could be asked whether it was fair for God to allow Job to go through all of the suffering in the first place. After all, Job was a very good man and someone God knew loved Him a great deal. Obviously, only God knows the exact reasons. I can think of two possible answers for why God allowed the suffering to come to Job.

One possible reason is God wanted Job to come to a greater understanding of who He was. After his encounter with God and fielding all of the questions from God, Job's knowledge and love for God grew tremendously. He understood to a greater depth than before just how awesome God really is. One of the most comforting verses in the Bible to Christians during difficult times is found in Romans.

And we know that in all things God works for the good of those who love him, who have been called according to his purpose.

(Romans 8:28)

This verse promises that if we love God then we can take comfort that what comes our way has been allowed by God and good will come from it. I have heard it said if you are a Christian and something "bad" happens in your life, the question should not be, "Why God did you allow this to happen to me?" The question to God should instead be, "What do you want me to learn from this?"

In Job's case he learned a lot more about God and how nothing escapes God's attention. He could take comfort in the fact that God is in absolute control of everything that takes place on His earth.

Another possible reason for God allowing the suffering to come Job's way is God knew that Job would withstand the attack from Satan. Throughout all of the suffering, while Job did have some questions for God about his situation, he never cursed God as Satan felt sure he would do, nor did he ever doubt the existence of God. The bottom line is Job's faith in God was real and it was deep. His faithfulness has been an inspiration for many Christians as they struggle with hardships.

If you are reading this chapter and you have experienced a great deal of heartache and suffering in your life, the first question to ask is whether the suffering is because of sin. You may realize that in fact a lot of the heartache in your life is a result of sin. The bad news is the past can not be changed but the good news is God is ready to offer forgiveness for any sins you have committed.

It may be, however, that even though you know you are a sinner and far from perfect, you do not really think you have done anything to warrant the pain and suffering you have experienced. I hope you realize that God loves you and He has a plan for you just like He did for the blind man and Job. I hope you will consider moving past any anger or unbelief of God and turning your heart to Him. It could be that God wants you to use your testimony to help many other people in similar situations to yours in order to lead them to Him.

In summary, only God knows why the particular man we read about was born blind and only God knows why He allowed Job to suffer so much. Both men ended up learning so much about God through their difficult circumstances, and their testimonies continue to bring glory to God. Only God knows why you have experienced all that you have. The thing you can be assured of is God knows everything about your life up to this point and He has a plan for the rest of your life that will bring glory to Him if you will just turn your heart to Him. Just like the blind man and Job, you have the opportunity to experience God and learn wonderful things about Him. The question is, are you going to seek God and open up your heart to Him?

I ALREADY HAVE A RELIGION

There are so many religions today. Therefore, one could easily say I already have a religion so I do not need Christianity. Up to this point I have used religion and Christianity interchangeably. However, there is a huge difference between religion and Christianity.

One of the best explanations of a key difference between religion and Christianity that I have come across is from Bob Mumford's book, *The Agape Road*. In this book, Mr. Mumford says the following, "The difference between religion and Christianity is: Religion is man seeking God. Christianity is God seeking man."

I know that the subject of religion is a very touchy one. I am definitely not an expert on the religions of the world and I have no desire whatsoever to try and tear down any religion. My only purpose in writing this book is to try and get people who are not Christians to at least consider if there is any validity in the belief that Jesus is the only way to Heaven. I truly feel that if someone genuinely desires to know if Jesus is the only way to Heaven, God will open their heart to His truth. In this chapter I am simply going to try and show why I believe that Jesus is the only way to Heaven.

In today's society the word sin is almost a forgotten word. Many words are used in place of sin. Some of these words are mistakes, failures, a lapse in judgment, or a weakness. It seems to be hard for people to even say the word sin. We would much rather say "I made a mistake" than say "I sinned". It is also hard for us many times to take full responsibility for our actions. We usually offer up reasons why we did something wrong in an attempt to justify our actions, such as saying such things as "I was just having a bad day" or "I didn't mean to say it but he just makes me so mad." This desire to try and justify our sins instead of taking full responsibility for them has been evident from the very first sin ever committed by man.

When God created the first man and woman, Adam and Eve, and put them in the Garden of Eden, He gave them instructions that there was one tree in the Garden which He called the tree of knowledge that they were not allowed to eat from. Satan disguised as a serpent, tempted Eve to eat the fruit from the tree that God had forbidden. Eve gave in to the temptation and then she gave some of the fruit to Adam and he also ate some. Notice how each of them explained their actions to God.

> The man said, "The woman you put here with me—she gave me some fruit from the tree and I ate it." Then the Lord God said to the woman, "What is this you have done?" The woman said, "The serpent deceived me, and I ate."
>
> (Genesis 3:12–13)

Adam pointed out that Eve gave him the fruit implying that it was her fault for offering him the apple. Notice Adam was also blaming God by reminding God that He was the one who put Eve in the Garden to be with him. In other words, if God had not created Eve then Adam would not be in the situation he was now in. He was doing his best to explain away his actions by blaming someone else. Of course, Eve immediately blamed the serpent.

The major problem with sin is it separates us from God who is perfect and holy.

> I am the Lord your God; consecrate yourselves and be holy, because I am holy.
>
> (Leviticus 11:44)

Adam and Eve had a perfect relationship with God before their sin. God would visit them in the Garden and I am sure Adam and Eve looked forward to those visits. However, after they sinned they hid from God when He came to visit them. Their relationship with God was broken because of their disobedience.

One of the greatest prophets of the Bible is Isaiah. God called Isaiah to be a prophet by giving him a vision.

> In the year that King Uzziah died, I saw the Lord seated on a throne, high and exalted, and the train of his robe filled the temple.
>
> (Isaiah 6:1)

Isaiah went on to describe the awesome sights and sounds that he witnessed. The result of his encounter had a very powerful impact on Isaiah and caused him to come to an important realization.

> "Woe to me!" I cried. "I am ruined! For I am a man of unclean lips, and I live among a people of unclean lips, and my eyes have seen the King, the Lord Almighty."
>
> (Isaiah 6:5)

Isaiah realized as he was in the presence of God just how holy God was and how sinful he was. You can feel the pain and fear in his message of "Woe to me" and "I am ruined".

Sin is anything that would be against the will of God and violates His holiness. If I lie or cheat that would be a sin. The Bible tells us very clearly that every person has a sin problem.

For all have sinned and fall short of the glory of God.

(Romans 3:23)

Man then has a dilemma. How can I take care of my sin problem and be in a right relationship with God? In other words, how can I keep from being ruined? Some people seem to feel that if they are a "good person" and do a lot of good things then their works will pay for their sins. It is like a see-saw and you just want to make sure that the good works side outweighs the sin side. I think there is a major flaw and concern with that understanding.

First of all, do we understand in God's eyes when something is really a sin? For example, we would probably all agree that adultery is a sin. Jesus indicated that even thinking about committing adultery is also a sin.

You have heard that it was said, 'Do not commit adultery,' But I tell you that anyone who looks at a woman lustfully has already committed adultery with her in his heart.

(Matthew 5:27–28)

How can we know then if we have done enough good works to off-set our sins if the way God looks at sin is a lot stricter than what we would consider a sin? It seems it would be impossible to keep score and we would live in fear and doubt our whole life of whether our good works were greater than our sins. The reality is we do not really need to keep score because just one sin makes us a sinner, separates us from God, and results in us needing a Savior.

Jesus made a very special promise to us that can take away the fear, doubt, and anxiety we have in our souls about whether we have the right relationship with God.

> Come to me, all you who are weary and burdened, and I will give you rest. Take my yoke upon you and learn from me, for I am gentle and humble in heart, and you will find rest for your souls. For my yoke is easy and my burden is light.
>
> (Matthew 11:28–30)

Once we accept Christ, we do not have to worry anymore about whether we have been good enough to get to Heaven. We will have the peace of knowing that we are going to Heaven because of what Jesus did on the cross and not because of anything we did. Jesus wants us to turn to Him so that He can remove the anxiety, burden, and worry about what will happen to us after we die. We will have rest for our souls because we will know we can trust the promises He makes to us once we accept Him.

The familiar verse below very simply explains the key to unlocking the doors of Heaven.

> For God so loved the world that he gave his one and only Son, that whoever believes in him shall not perish but have eternal life.
>
> (John 3:16)

Later in the same book of the Bible Jesus reminds us once again that He is the only way to Heaven.

I am the way and the truth and the life. No one comes to the Father except through me.

(John 14:6)

The bottom line is we have to make a decision about whether Jesus is telling us the truth or not. In the Old Testament book of Isaiah there is lot of prophesy about Jesus and how His sacrifice on the cross would be the way for all men to be forgiven for their sins and have a right relationship with God.

But he was pierced for our transgressions, he was crushed for our iniquities; the punishment that brought us peace was upon him, and by his wounds we are healed.

(Isaiah 53:5)

The one being talked about in this verse is Jesus. God's plan from the beginning of His creation was to allow Jesus to come to His earth and be the sacrifice for the sins of all men because Jesus was the only perfect man. Notice the verse highlights that our relationship with God is healed and the resulting peace we have is because Jesus paid the price for our sins by allowing himself to be pierced and crushed. He accepted our punishment which shows how much He loves us. We simply have to confess to God that yes, I am a sinner and I need a Savior. For many people that sounds too easy and surely we need to do something more than simply confess our sins and believe in Jesus as our Savior and Lord.

When someone says, "I need to do something to get to Heaven," notice where their focus is. Their focus is

still on self. In order to really be in the right relationship with God, our focus has to shift away from ourselves
to the Lord Jesus. We have to realize that we can't pay
for our sins. However, we can put our trust and faith in
someone who can take care of them for us. In order for
Jesus to be our Lord, our focus has to shift to Him.

What does the verse really mean when it says we
must "believe" in Jesus? It is not simply saying with words
that we believe in Him. The belief in Christ that is the
saving belief comes directly from the heart. When someone truly believes in something with all of their heart, it
means they are willing to sacrifice for it because they feel
so strongly about it.

> Therefore, I urge you, brothers, in view of God's
> mercy, to offer your bodies as living sacrifices, holy
> and pleasing to God–that is your spiritual act of
> worship.
>
> (Romans 12:1)

This type of a belief is recognizing that Christ loves
us so much that He died on the cross to pay for our sins.
Our belief in Him should mean that we desire to please
Him by obeying His teachings and commandments. It
means trusting Him completely and worshipping Him
by being a "living sacrifice". It means giving up control
of our lives to Him. The next chapter will go in greater
detail about what it means to give up control of our life
to Jesus.

Why do so many people have a problem with Jesus
being the only way to Heaven? I think one possible
answer to that question is our human nature. We love to

think "there is more than one way to skin a cat." We like to have choices. Advertisers love to point out the flexibility of their products because they know that people like to have options.

If ten people set out to drive from Point A to Point B they would probably come up with several different routes. Some would want to go the fastest way. Others may enjoy sightseeing and take a lot of back roads in order to enjoy their trip more. The bottom line is we like to have options and quite frankly we tend to get upset when we are told something has to be a certain way. Therefore, I think that is why a lot of people are turned off by hearing Jesus is the only way to Heaven. We tend to immediately become defiant and ask, "What do you mean the only way?" One of the popular criticisms of Christians is they are closed minded because of their belief that Jesus is the only way to Heaven.

Wouldn't a perfect God come up with the perfect way for people to have salvation? Why would He have multiple options when He knows the best option? Think about the positives of Jesus being the only way to Heaven. First of all, we do not have to possess any special kind of skills to have salvation. We simply have to accept the gift of salvation that is offered. Remember the key words of John 3:16: "that whoever believes in him." It takes no special abilities to believe in something. Every person has the ability to believe and have faith. Also, notice there are not any restrictions on who can believe in Jesus. Whoever does not exclude anyone.

If we could get to Heaven based on our works, think about how people would be in Heaven. We would be feeling prideful about our accomplishment of getting to

Heaven. Once again our focus would be on self and our accomplishments.

> For it is by grace you have been saved, through faith—and this is not from yourselves, it is the gift of God—not by works, so that no one can boast.
>
> (Ephesians 2:8–9)

Instead, with God's plan, when we get to Heaven we will be so thankful to God for what He did for us that praising Him will come naturally. Our focus will be exactly where it should be, which will be on our Heavenly Father.

If your religion does not believe that Jesus is the only way to Heaven, then I realize how hard it is to question something you have been taught and believed in your entire life. There was a man in the Bible named Nicodemus who realized that he needed to find out the truth about Jesus for himself and not just listen to his religious leaders.

> Now there was a man of the Pharisees named Nicodemus, a member of the Jewish ruling council. He came to Jesus at night and said, "Rabbi, we know you are a teacher who has come from God. For no one could perform the miraculous signs you are doing if God were not with him." In reply Jesus declared, "I tell you the truth, no one can see the kingdom of God unless he is born again."
>
> (John 3:1–3)

Jesus went on to explain to Nicodemus what He

meant by the term born again. Nicodemus was a Pharisee and a member of the Jewish ruling council. This group was opposing Jesus because they were jealous of the attention He was receiving, and also because Jesus was not shy about letting them know how hypocritical they were. Obviously, Nicodemus could not just fall in line with the others and oppose Jesus because he realized there was something very special about Jesus because of the powerful miracles He was performing. Notice it says that he came at night and that was probably because he did not want anyone to know what he was doing. Nicodemus obviously had doubts about Jesus but he decided he needed to find out the truth for himself.

Hopefully, you feel motivated to also find out the truth about Jesus for yourself. Some practical ways to get started will be covered in the last chapter.

GIVING UP CONTROL OF MY LIFE

Some people have not totally ignored the issue of Jesus and Christianity. However, the commitment and sacrifice to Christ scares them. They wonder about the changes that may take place in their life. When you read the Bible, you will find that Jesus is very upfront and clear about what He expects from someone who is a Christian. Jesus expects His believers to trust Him. Also, He expects to be the number one priority in our lives and He expects our focus to be on Him and not on ourselves. Notice Jesus' message in the following verses:

When Jesus saw the crowd around him, he gave
orders to cross to the other side of the lake. Then a
teacher of the law came to him and said, "Teacher,
I will follow you wherever you go." Jesus replied,
"Foxes have holes and birds of the air have nests,
but the Son of Man has no place to lay his head."
Another disciple said to him, "Lord, first let me go
and bury my father." But Jesus told him, "Follow
me, and let the dead bury their own dead."

(Matthew 8:18–22)

These verses will scare a lot of people. We like to have
assurances or promises about the future if we commit
to do something. Jesus is letting us know that following Him means we will have to trust Him from day to
day. Jesus' response to the man about burying his father
seems to conflict with the Bible teaching that we are to
"honor thy father and thy mother." I think the message
He is sending us is we are to put being obedient to Him
as our top priority. He will then direct us and His direction will be consistent with all of His commandments.

The constant struggle every Christian faces is doing
what Christ wants us to do versus doing what we want
to do. Jesus tells us very clearly that following Him will
require that we deny self.

Then Jesus said to his disciples, "If anyone would
come after me, he must deny himself and take up his
cross and follow me.

(Matthew 16:24)

Denying self simply means doing what Jesus wants

us to do instead of what we would like to do. For example, when someone hurts us we like to return the favor by hurting them. We view it almost as a right to get even with them. Jesus wants us to forgive them and not to retaliate. We have to deny ourselves the "pleasure" of getting even if we want to please Jesus.

Denying self also involves sacrificing our comfort and selfish interests for the benefit of others. Time is a precious commodity. It is the one thing that people have in common. Some people have more money and possessions but no one has more than twenty-four hours in a day. Serving Jesus and helping others requires that we give up some of our time devoted to our own selfish interests in order to assist others. When you think about it, the greatest way to show someone you love them is by investing time in them which usually involves denying oneself. The absolute best way to show Jesus you love Him is by following His command to help others. He constantly talked to His disciples about helping people, especially the poor and anyone that was in need.

For example, both of my sons are avid golfers and played on their high school golf teams. During their high school years our church went on mission trips to Haiti and Honduras during their spring breaks. The work was always hard and the climates were extremely hot. It would have been a lot more enjoyable for them to play golf during that week. However, the work was providing homes to people that had very little and while they were denying their own selfish interests, both of them will tell you the experiences were well worth it.

Our church provides our old parsonage to missionary families when they come back to the United States between missionary assignments. Two of the missionary families that stayed in our parsonage recently are great examples of being obedient to Jesus. Both of these families were called to the missionary field after they were adults. They had children, nice homes, and good jobs. However, both couples felt the call of the Lord to become missionaries. They investigated what the process was in becoming missionaries and they decided to be obedient to God's calling to be missionaries. They did not know where they would be serving or exactly what they would be doing. The only things they knew were they would be doing what Christ wanted them to do and they could trust Him. Today both families are serving in foreign countries sharing the good news of Jesus Christ and the salvation that He offers. You do not have to be around these families very long before you are struck with the sense of how joyful and content they are.

I know when some people hear about commitments like these missionaries made, it bothers them. They wonder if they become a Christian what changes may be required of them. I have always been amazed at how change is viewed by people. We love to complain about the way things are. However, when changes are proposed, we are quick to become negative about the changes. I guess we are simply afraid the changes will make things worse instead of better. The truth is when God is leading us to make a change it will always be for the better.

I would like to share from the Bible why turning over control of our lives to Christ is absolutely the best thing we can do. First of all, each person born is a unique and special person. It amazes me how with all the people there are in the world every person's fingerprints are unique. We are told in Psalm about our creation.

> For you created my inmost being; you knit me together in my mother's womb. I praise you because I am fearfully and wonderfully made; your works are wonderful, I know that full well.
>
> (Psalm 139:13–14)

It is awesome to know people are never an accident and it is also assuring to know that God has a plan for each one of us. His plan for us involves us joining with Him in doing His work and He has equipped us with the ability to be successful in whatever He desires for us to do.

> For we are God's workmanship created in Christ Jesus to do good works, which God prepared in advance for us to do.
>
> (Ephesians 2:10)

God, in speaking to the Israelites while they were held captive by the Babylonians, made a very special promise to them. The Israelites had a history of turning away from God, suffering the consequences, then repenting of their sins, and turning back to God. In this particular instance God made a very comforting statement to them.

"For I know the plans I have for you," declares the

> Lord, "plans to prosper you and not to harm you,
> plans to give you a hope and a future."
>
> (Jeremiah 29:11)

I believe with all of my heart that is God's promise to us today. We are here for a reason. Our Creator knows us better than we even know ourselves. He has a specific purpose for our being on this Earth at this particular time. He knows that we will only be fulfilled and satisfied if we commit our lives to Him and accomplish the purposes we were created for. That is why I feel the two missionary families mentioned earlier are so content. They are exactly where God wants them and doing what God wants them to do.

I can hear someone saying that sounds good, but what about all the Christians who have died for their faith. There are missionaries today who are still being killed for sharing their faith. How can that fit with God's promise "to prosper you and not to harm you"?

The Bible offers a great answer to that question. Consider the very first Christian martyr. His name was Stephen. He was arrested because of his faith and in his defense he shared how Jesus was the Messiah, the Savior that the Jewish people had been looking for. He also let them know they were guilty of killing the Savior. The people were furious when they heard what Stephen was telling them.

> When they heard this, they were furious and gnashed
> their teeth at him. But Stephen, full of the Holy
> Spirit, looked up to heaven, and saw the glory of
> God, and Jesus standing at the right hand of God.

"Look," he said, "I see heaven open and the Son of Man standing at the right hand of God."

(Acts 7:54–56)

They proceeded to stone Stephen to death. But notice what it says about how he died.

While they were stoning him, Stephen prayed, "Lord Jesus, receive my spirit." Then he fell on his knees and cried out, "Lord do not hold this sin against them." When he had said this, he fell asleep. And Saul was there, giving approval to his death.

(Acts 7:59–60)

Do you see what an awesome thing God did for Stephen? He opened up Heaven and let Stephen see exactly where he was headed. He saw the glory of God and Jesus standing at the right hand of God. He knew that everything he believed and had been sharing with others was the absolute truth. There was no way Stephen feared death now. I can almost imagine him wanting them to hurry up and stone him so that he could get to Heaven.

Stephen also asked God to forgive the people who were stoning him. That is exactly what Jesus did when He was crucified. After Jesus was placed on the cross and the men who placed Him there were dividing up Jesus' clothes, Jesus asked God to forgive them. Stephen truly was obedient to Jesus' teachings to the very end of his life.

Stephen made a choice to become a Christian. He also decided he was going to be faithful to Christ even though it would result in him being killed. The key point is he had choices to make. The fact that God has always given man the opportunity to decide if he wants to be obedient or not is an indication of the relationship God desires to have with us.

When God put Adam and Eve in the Garden of Eden, He told them as we discussed in the last chapter that they could not eat from one tree.

> And the Lord God commanded the man, "You are free to eat from any tree in the garden; but you must not eat from the tree of the knowledge of good and evil, for when you eat of it you will surely die."
>
> (Genesis 2:16–17)

Unfortunately, Adam and Eve did eat from that tree and sin was introduced into the world. Why did God have that tree in the Garden? Would it not have been better to leave the tree out of the Garden so that they could not be disobedient? God did not create man to be a puppet who did not have freedom of choice. Instead He wants us to worship Him and give up control of our life to Him because we love Him and we choose to do so.

So have you been afraid of Christianity because you do not want to give up any control of your life and you are also afraid of what it might "cost" you? The real question is why were you created? What did God intend for you to do with your life? What is it going to really cost you if you do not find out what your purpose is?

We can be absolutely certain we will never be complete, satisfied, and at peace until we decide to commit our life to Christ and discover our purpose. Living for that purpose will make life real because for the first time we are living the way God intended for us to live. Also, accepting Christ and getting to know Him in an intimate way will result in us knowing we can trust Him which will provide us a great deal of comfort and peace.

Whatever specific purpose planned by God for us is good and we can know we are qualified to accomplish it because it is what God intended for us to do. I can look at my life to provide some examples that these statements are true.

In high school I was a very shy person. I absolutely hated to get up in front of the class to give any type of report and my extremely sweaty hands were proof of how nervous I was. Math was my best subject and English was my worst subject. Writing papers was not something I enjoyed or something I was very good at. One of the most embarrassing moments of my life was in the tenth grade. My English teacher decided to put one of my papers on the overhead to critique it. She covered up my name and did not say whose paper it was. Well that particular paper brought a lot of laughs from the class. The laughs were not because the paper was funny. The laughs were because the paper was poorly written. That was the longest class of my life and I never thought the bell was going to ring. Finally, the girl that sat beside me could sense that I wasn't enjoying the paper as much as everyone else and asked if it was my paper. I lied and said no.

I point out those things to show what God can do. Today I teach a Sunday School class of around fifty people. If you had told me in high school that one day I would enjoy standing up in front of a class and lead Bible studies, I would have thought you were crazy. If you then told me that one day I would write a book that would have sealed the deal that you had lost your mind.

However, after accepting Christ, He started to reveal things to me that He wanted me to do. I am amazed where He has led me and I am excited about where He will continue to lead. By giving up control of our life to Christ we are able to accomplish things far beyond our expectations because we are no longer relying on our strength but instead we now have His strength and power in our lives.

I can do everything through him who gives me strength.

(Philippians 4:13)

I know that I can trust Jesus when I face death. I know that He will be in Heaven still at the right hand of God and will be waiting for me just like He was there for Stephen. So please do not let the fear of change keep you from being open to Christ. Yes, accepting Christ will bring changes in your life. However, these changes will not be "costs"; instead they will be "benefits". You will find that these changes are things that you really want to do. God is not going to lead you to make changes without supplying both the desire and ability to make those changes.

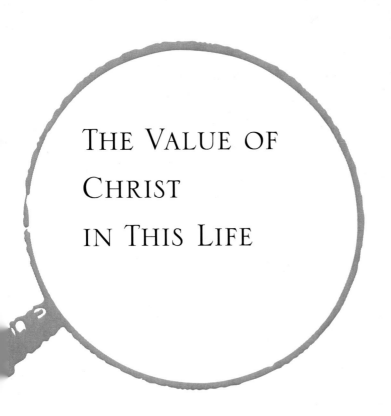

THE VALUE OF CHRIST IN THIS LIFE

When I accepted Christ in 1982, my focus was on my need to have Jesus as my Savior so that when I died I would be able to go to Heaven. I understood and believed that He was the only way to Heaven. I also understood that I would need to live like a Christian although at that point I was not exactly sure what that meant. I viewed God as being concerned about the big and important things of my life. I have been surprised to discover after becoming a Christian how much value Christ brings to my life on this Earth and how involved He can be in every aspect of my life if only I will allow Him to be. I now understand that God is concerned about every detail of my life and no detail is too small for Him because He wants to develop me in order to use me for His purposes.

After Jesus was crucified and resurrected, He gave His disciples and believers a command before He ascended back into Heaven.

> On one occasion, while he was eating with them, he gave them this command: "Do not leave Jerusalem, but wait for the gift my Father promised, which you have heard me speak about. For John baptized with water, but in a few days you will be baptized with the Holy Spirit."
>
> (Acts 1:4–5)

Once we accept Christ, the Holy Spirit comes into our life. The trinity of God is the Father, the Son, and the Holy Spirit. Jesus on several occasions shared with His disciples that He was God.

> Jesus answered: "Don't you know me, Philip, even after I have been among you such a long time? Anyone who has seen me has seen the Father. How can you say, 'Show us the Father'? Don't you believe that I am in the Father and that the Father is in me? The words I say to you are not just my own. Rather, it is the Father, living in me, who is doing his work.
>
> (John 14:9–10)

The Holy Spirit is God just like Jesus is God. A Christian has the Spirit of God in their lives and the

Holy Spirit will be working to convict us of our sins and to change us for the better.

Max Lucado in his book, *Just Like Jesus,* makes a statement that I feel is very true. He says, "God loves you just the way you are, but he refuses to leave you that way. More than anything, he wants you to be just like Jesus." We do not have to do anything in order to gain God's love. He loves each one of us with no conditions attached. He wants each one of us to accept Jesus just like we are, which will result in the Holy Spirit coming into our life, and then the Holy Spirit will begin working to help us become more like Jesus in both our actions and in our relationship with the Father.

> ...for it is God who works in you to will and to act according to his good purpose.
>
> (Philippians 2:13)

The problem after we accept Christ and the Holy Spirit comes into our life is we still have our old selfish ways and desires within us as well. The spiritual warfare between our old self that is focused on what we desire to do versus what the Holy Spirit desires for us to do begins. I wish I could say it is easy to always do what we know the Holy Spirit is leading us to do. Unfortunately, the battles are not easy and even though we have the Holy Spirit within us, many times we let our selfish desires win some or a lot of the battles. That is why, as was mentioned in the chapter on hypocritical Christians, that some may conclude that Christianity has no value because they see so many examples of Christians who sin.

The Bible very clearly indicates the battle that wages within.

> So I say, live by the Spirit, and you will not gratify the desires of the sinful nature. For the sinful nature desires what is contrary to the Spirit, and the Spirit what is contrary to the sinful nature. They are in conflict with each other, so that you do not do what you want.
>
> (Galatians 5:16–17)

You may be saying I do not want this battle waging in me all the time, so what could possibly be the value of Christ on Earth. The value is we have the ammunition through the Holy Spirit to start winning some of the battles. Our selfish and sinful nature is always going to lead us to do what benefits us the most and to do what is the most convenient thing for us to do. The Holy Spirit will challenge us to do what God wants us to do which many times will be exactly the opposite of what our selfish nature desires for us to do. The real battle that is waging within us is whether we trust God enough to follow His instructions and not our selfish desires. The great thing is when we allow the Holy Spirit to defeat our old sinful nature we begin to discover we can trust God and experience a new joy that we have never experienced before. It then becomes a little easier to listen to the Holy Spirit the next time we face a battle.

One of my favorite examples in the Bible of trusting God is found in the book of Daniel. Many of the Israelites had been deported to Babylon. Three young men who were deported were Shadrach, Meshach, and

Abednego. They were ordered by King Nebuchadnezzar to bow down and worship an image of gold that the king had set up. The three young men refused to worship the idol because doing so would violate one of the Ten Commandments. The King told them if they did not worship the image of gold they would be thrown in a blazing furnace. Notice the response of the three men.

> Shadrach, Meshach, and Abednego replied to the king, "O Nebuchadnezzar, we do not need to defend ourselves before you in this matter. If we are thrown into the blazing furnace, the God we serve is able to save us from it, and he will rescue us from your hand, O king. But even if he does not we want you to know, O king, that we will not serve your gods or worship the image of gold that you set up.
>
> (Daniel 3:16–18)

Of course, their response made King Nebuchadnezzar furious, and he ordered the three men to be thrown into the furnace. When the King looked into the fire he was amazed at what he saw.

> Then King Nebuchadnezzar leaped to his feet in amazement and asked his advisers, "Weren't there three men that we tied up and threw into the fire?" They replied, "Certainly, O King." He said, "Look! I see four men walking around in the fire, unbound, and unharmed, and the fourth looks like a son of the gods."
>
> (Daniel 3:24–25)

He then told them to come out of the fire and proceeded to praise their God. Who was the fourth man? Many people speculate it was Jesus or an angel there protecting them.

It would have been very easy for the three young men to decide to worship the image of gold. They could have reasoned that they could not serve God if they were killed, and was it really going to hurt anything by bowing down to the image. The fire had to be intimidating and I am sure their flesh was begging them to take the easy way out. However, they decided they were going to trust God. What an incredible experience with God they would have missed if they had caved in to the King's wishes. Do you think it was easier the next time they faced a situation where they had to choose whether to be obedient to God or not?

Please note the benefits that resulted from the three young men's obedience to God. They brought honor to God by their willingness to die for Him. Their obedience benefited others because it revealed to them who God is and that He is the one and only true God. Finally, they personally received a tremendous blessing during this encounter as they experienced God and His love for them.

I truly believe God has a purpose for every person born. In order to learn what our purpose is, we have to accept Christ as our Savior and allow the Holy Spirit to work in our lives by being obedient to His guidance. The journey will not be easy and we will be tested as we learn to trust following the Holy Spirit's instructions and not what our selfish desires tell us. By being obedient to the Holy Spirit and not our own selfish desires, we will begin to experience God in a very personal, intimate, and powerful way which is the greatest thing about Christianity in this life.

There are numerous other advantages of knowing Christ in this life that are very practical things that make our life on this earth more peaceful and joyful. For example, we can become more forgiving, learn to worry less, and we have a resource to provide direction when we have important decisions to make.

I have heard it said that we never look more like Christ than when we forgive. After all, that is exactly what He did for us. Our sins were forgiven because of the price that Christ paid on the cross. Jesus indicated on numerous occasions that we should be a continually forgiving person.

> Then Peter came to Jesus and asked, "Lord, how many times shall I forgive my brother when he sins against me? Up to seven times?" Jesus answered, "I tell you, not seven times, but seventy-seven times."
>
> (Matthew 18:21–22)

> "If he sins against you seven times in a day, and seven times comes back to you and says, 'I repent ,' forgive him."
>
> (Luke 17:4)

Obviously, Jesus wants Christians to be a very forgiving people. It seems almost impossible to think about forgiving a person seven times in one day, especially when we struggle to forgive them once. Jesus also gives a very stern warning if we choose to not forgive.

"For if you forgive men when they sin against you, your heavenly Father will also forgive you. But if you do not forgive men their sins, your Father will not forgive your sins."

(Matthew 6:14–15)

I can think of three primary reasons why God stresses for us to forgive so much. First of all, anytime we sin, while we may be hurting someone else, we are sinning against God. As we have learned, a major part of accepting Christ is confessing that I am a sinner in the eyes of God, and I need a Savior so that my sins will be forgiven. Therefore, when someone else sins against us, they are also sinning against God. God wants us to forgive them just like He will do if they will confess and repent. If we do not forgive them then we are saying their sins against me are greater than their sins against God. This attitude is reflecting that our focus is on self and not on God. When we do forgive others, we are honoring God and showing our love for Him.

A second reason why I think God stresses forgiveness so much is the powerful witness it can be to someone else. When we forgive it will undoubtedly surprise some people and they may be curious why and how we could forgive the other person. It is a great opportunity to then share with them that it is because of Jesus that we can forgive. I recently saw the movie, *End of the Spear,* about a group of missionaries who were killed in Ecuador. Their families, instead of seeking revenge, forgave the Indians who killed the men and continued to reach out to the Indians. The forgiveness of the families was a major witness to the Indians and a real factor in leading them to Christ.

Finally, I think God wants us to forgive because He knows that is what is best for us. When we do not forgive, we can become very bitter and spiteful. I have heard it said that when we do not forgive someone then they end up hurting us twice because of the pain and anger we allow to remain in us. Tragically, the second hurt can be much worse than the original hurt because it can result in ruining all of our joy and peace.

Do you see all of the positives that result when we forgive as Jesus wants us to do? First of all, we honor God by submitting to His will and not our own. We also benefit other people around us by being a positive witness for Christ. Finally, we personally receive a benefit because our obedience keeps us from bringing harm to ourselves.

Notice these are the exact same benefits that resulted when Shadrach, Meshach, and Abednego were obedient to God. Living for God and being obedient to Jesus' commands will always result in God being honored, others being enlightened about the ways of God, and we will also be blessed in some way. Those benefits would seem to add a great deal of value to anyone's life.

One area that I have struggled with for most of my life is worrying. Jesus numerous times in the Bible tells us not to worry.

Then Jesus said to his disciples: "Therefore, I tell you, do not worry about your life, what you will eat; or about your body, what you will wear. Life is more than food, and the body more than clothes.

Consider the ravens: They do not sow or reap, they have no storeroom or barn; yet God feeds them. And how much more valuable you are than birds! Who of you by worrying can add a single hour to his life? Since you cannot do this very little thing, why do you worry about the rest?"

(Luke 12:22–26)

The real message we send when we worry is we are saying that we cannot completely trust God about every aspect of our life. God makes a very special promise to His believers in the book of Romans.

And we know that in all things God works for the good of those who love him, who have been called according to his purpose.

(Romans 8:28)

This verse brings a lot of comfort to believers during times of trouble because it is a reminder that God is in control of all things, He is always at work, He loves us, and He has our best interests at heart. A great example to illustrate the truth of this verse is found when Jesus was crucified. Jesus' disciples understood Jesus was the Messiah but they were thinking He was going to set up an Earthly kingdom. They never quite grasped what Jesus was telling them about how He had to die. Therefore, their world was shattered when Jesus was crucified. Their dreams were crushed and they had also lost their friend, leader, and mentor. It would probably have been impossible to convince them the night after Jesus died that good was going to come from Jesus being crucified. Of course, three days later Jesus was resurrected and then the disciples slowly started to understand the meaning of everything that had happened. Actually, Jesus' death was the best news ever for mankind because His perfect sacrifice paves the way for each one of us to be in the right relationship with God.

Therefore, if we belong to Christ, we can take great comfort in the fact that God is in control and we have to trust Him during difficult times that good will come of it. Many times our difficulties will result in us becoming closer to God as we search for comfort and maybe even answers. Anything that results in us becoming closer to God is a good thing.

The closer we become to God and the more we begin to understand His love the more security we have in Him. Therefore, our relationship with God will result in us worrying less. Many people need an answer to their problem of worrying and the only answer comes from knowing Christ.

The Bible is God's love letter and instruction book to man. It can help us make decisions that we face from day to day. Sometimes the Bible is just a reminder to make decisions that would please God, such as choosing not to cheat in order to obtain something we want. Following God's instructions about unwavering honesty and integrity are important. God does not condone the philosophy "it is only wrong if you get caught." He wants us to follow His commands because it is what is best for us and will keep us from bringing trouble to ourselves.

There are other times when we are trying to make a decision where we are not sure what the correct decision is because it not a decision between right and wrong. For example, I was once faced with making a career decision about taking a new job. I was really torn about what to do and finally one morning before my quiet time in God's word I prayed to God asking Him to reveal to me through His word if I should pursue the job change or not. I opened my Bible and started reading Hebrews 13 because that is where I left off the previous morning. Notice verse 5.

> Keep your lives free from the love of money and be content with what you have, because God has said, "Never will I leave you: never will I forsake you."
>
> (Hebrews 13:5)

As soon as I finished reading those words, I knew God was letting me know it was best for me to stay in my current job and to be content with what I had. Was it just some coincidence that I happened to be reading that morning that particular scripture verse? I would tell you no. God loves me, He knows the future, and He also knows me. I know that I can trust Him and His direction. I had a peace about what I needed to do and there was no second guessing the decision. I am not sure why the other job was not right for me because it seemed like the perfect job for me in so many ways. I just trusted that God knew something about the job that I did not know and it was best for me at that moment to remain in my current job.

Does God always give an immediate and clear answer like He did for me that particular morning? No, He does not. Sometimes we have to be persistent and continually seek His direction. I think the delay is sometimes because He wants to teach us something during the search-ing process. The bottom line is God's word needs to be our primary resource as we attempt to make decisions.

You may be wondering exactly how accepting Christ is going to help you to become a more forgiving person who worries less. Part of that answer quite frankly is beyond our understanding.

> Rejoice in the Lord always. I will say it again: Rejoice! Let your gentleness be evident to all. The Lord is near. Do not be anxious about anything, but in ev-erything, by prayer and petition, with thanksgiving, present your requests to God. And the peace of God, which transcends all understanding, will guard your hearts and your minds in Christ Jesus.
>
> (Philippians 4:4–7)

Remember, when we accept Christ, we receive the Holy Spirit which means God is part of us. He will be working in us to help us make choices that please Him. We should have a desire to please God if we have truly accepted Jesus as our Savior and Lord. Jesus indicated that there is a very simple test to determine if we love Him.

> Jesus replied, "If anyone loves me, he will obey my teaching. My Father will love him, and we will come to him and make our home with him.
>
> (John 14:23)

While having the desire to obey God is important and a necessary first step, what really matters is are we

actually obedient in our actions. Every time we are obedient to God we draw closer to Him, we learn about
Him, and we discover we can trust Him. Notice this
verse indicates God and Jesus will make their home with
us if we are obedient. It is almost like our obedience is
a welcome mat for God to truly take control of our life.
When we are obedient we find we change for the better.
We may not even understand how we can feel forgiveness or why we are not worried. The reason, as the verse
in Philippians points out, is because of the peace of God
which transcends all understanding is within us.

A great illustration of this peace that transcends
all understanding comes from one the members of our
Sunday School class. Notice the Monday she had a few
years ago. Her husband, who is a deputy sheriff, literally
had the end of one of his fingers bitten off by one of the
new police dogs that was in training. Her son punctured
the palm of his hand on a chain link fence at school.
On her way home from the hospital that evening, she
and her daughter were involved in a car accident, sending them back to the emergency room. Fortunately, there
were no injuries. That would definitely be labeled as a
bad Monday. The next Sunday as she was sharing her
Monday experiences with the class, she indicated that if
all of these things had happened a few years earlier before
becoming a Christian she would have been a "basket
case." Instead, she felt a peace that surprised her, and a
feeling that all these situations could not touch her.

In 1997, I went through a Bible study called
Experiencing God that was written by Henry T. Blackaby
and Claude V. King. I feel this study has probably had
the single greatest impact on my Christian growth. This

course revealed a large number of truths to me through the scripture. I would like to summarize some of these key truths. One of the great revelations that was driven home to me was the fact that God is always working around me. His desire is to have a love relationship with me and for me to become involved in His work with Him. If I will adjust my life so that I can join Him in His work and if I will be obedient to Him, then I can come to know God by experience. Think about the fact that God wants to involve us in His work on this Earth and we can then know Him by our experience with Him. Doesn't that seem like it would be an awfully exciting and fulfilling thing and make life on this Earth much more worthwhile?

If we are not living for God then we are living for self. Self is never satisfied. Self wants more money, more comfort, less problems, more recognition, etc. Self will never be content because there is always one more thing that self wants to have.

Is there value in living for Christ while living on this Earth? Absolutely. Are you tired of feeling angry, afraid, and unloved? Would you like to stop worrying and being so judgmental of other people? Would you like to have a joy and peace as you live each day? Would you like to know there is a real purpose for your life and would you like to experience God?

Accepting Christ will result in you being able to go to Heaven. Listening to the Holy Spirit and being obedient to His instructions will result in you growing in Christ. That growing process will be exciting, fulfilling, and extremely valuable.

STEPS FOR SEEKING THE TRUTH

My sincere hope if you are not a Christian is you have decided that you are going to pursue for yourself if Jesus is the only way to Heaven. This chapter will offer some advice on how to get started. My fear is you will end up doing nothing after reading this last chapter. You may decide that you are going to pursue the answer and then just never quite get around to doing it. The good news is I am confident that God will still be pursuing you.

Almost can be a very disappointing word. For example, if someone says their team almost won the game it means that they lost the game but it was close. Someone else may say I almost got the job but the reality is that they did not get it. There was an incident in the Bible when someone said they were almost persuaded to be a Christian.

Paul was arrested once because of his faith in Christ. Paul had the opportunity to speak to one of the Roman kings, King Agrippa. Paul gave a very clear description of how he became a Christian. He told how he fought against Christianity and then one day, on the road to Damascus, Jesus met him and he finally realized exactly who Jesus was. After listening to Paul's account, King Agrippa made the following statement.

> Then Agrippa said unto Paul, "Almost thou persuadest me to be a Christian."
>
> (Acts 26:28 KJV)

Hopefully at some point King Agrippa did become a Christian. The sad reality is if he died and was only almost persuaded to be a Christian then he died without being one. He then faced death with the weight of his sins on his shoulders since he did not have the blood of Jesus to wash away his sins and his eternal destination was Hell.

Jesus once painted a very clear picture of what a terrible place Hell is. Jesus told a story of a rich man who went to Hell. While in Hell this rich man was allowed to look into Heaven and he saw a poor beggar named Lazarus who used to stay outside the gate of his house. The beggar was in Heaven with Abraham. The rich man then begged Abraham to allow Lazarus to come and bring him some water because he was in agony in the fire. Abraham responded that it was not possible to go from Heaven to Hell because there was a barrier that was impossible to pass.

After receiving that answer the rich man had one more request.

> He answered, "Then I beg you, father, send Lazarus to my father's house, for I have five brothers. Let him warn them, so that they will not also come to this place of torment." Abraham replied, "They have Moses and the Prophets, let them listen to them." "No, father Abraham," he said, "but if someone from the dead goes to them, they will repent." He said to him, "If they do not listen to Moses and the Prophets, they will not be convinced even if someone rises from the dead."
>
> (Luke 16:27–31)

Hell is a terrible place, "a place of torment", and I do not want anyone to go there. I have heard people say, "If I go to Hell at least I will be with my friends." Friends will be no comfort whatsoever in Hell. If so, wouldn't the rich man have welcomed his brothers in Hell? Instead he wanted to make sure that they did not end up in Hell.

The rich man seemed very confident that if someone from the dead went to his brothers then they would repent. Jesus' reply is discouraging to the rich man. He said that if they would not listen to Moses and the prophets then they would not listen to someone who returned from the dead. Jesus made that statement of course knowing that He would soon be raised from the dead and yet people would still not believe in Him.

Unfortunately some people refuse to believe in Jesus no matter how much evidence there is to support that He is real and He truly is the Son of God.

Jesus knew while on Earth that people were not just going to believe Him because He said He was God's son. After all, anyone could make that claim. He knew people needed some proof.

> "What about the one whom the Father set apart as his very own and sent into the world? Why then do you accuse me of blasphemy because I said, 'I am God's Son? Do not believe me unless I do what my Father does. But if I do it, even though you do not believe me, believe the miracles, that you may know and understand that the Father is in me, and I in the Father."
>
> (John 10:36–38)

Jesus performed countless miracles of raising the dead, giving sight to the blind, making the lame walk, and healing people with terrible diseases. Notice what the last verse of the book of John says.

> Jesus did many other things as well. If every one of them were written down, I suppose that even the whole world would not have room for the books that would be written.
>
> (John 21:25)

In the four gospels about the ministry of Jesus we are told about many miracles performed by Jesus. Obviously, Jesus did many more besides the ones that are recorded.

It is easy to see why that would be the case. Jesus is very compassionate and He would reach out to help someone in need. Jesus also did the miracles to validate that He was the Son of the Father, the Messiah. Only God could do the miracles that Jesus was performing. A man who simply proclaimed to be God would not have the power to do the awesome miracles that Jesus did.

Peter, one of Jesus' closest disciples, wanted to assure everyone that Jesus was real because he had witnessed Jesus' miracles and teaching first hand.

> We did not follow cleverly invented stories when we told you about the power and coming of our Lord Jesus Christ, but we were eyewitnesses of his majesty.
>
> (2 Peter 1:16)

An eyewitness is very important in proving someone's innocence or guilt. Peter and many others were eyewitnesses of the countless examples that supported Jesus' claims of who He was. They saw His miracles and they also saw Him after He was resurrected.

After Jesus ascended back into Heaven, the Christians faced a lot of opposition and persecution because of their belief in Jesus. For example, once Peter and some other Christians were arrested. One of the teachers of the Jewish law, Gamaliel, then gave the following advice to the Jewish leaders opposing the Christian movement.

> "Therefore, in the present case I advise you: Leave these men alone! Let them go! For if their purpose or activity is of human origin, it will fail. But if it is

from God, you will not be able to stop these men; you will only find yourselves fighting against God."

(Acts 5:38–39)

I think that was great advice by Gamaliel. Here we are over two thousand years later and Christianity is still here because it is from God and it was His purpose from the beginning of His creation that Jesus would come to Earth and be the Savior for men.

You may be thinking it would be so easy for me to believe if I could physically see Jesus. After Jesus was resurrected, the news was shared with one of His disciples named Thomas that Jesus was alive. Thomas was skeptical and said he would not believe it until he saw Jesus for himself and put his fingers where the nails had been. Soon after this, Thomas did meet Jesus and Jesus told Thomas to put his fingers where the nails had been. Jesus then made the following statement to Thomas.

Then Jesus told him, "Because you have seen me, you have believed; blessed are those who have not seen and yet have believed."

(John 20:29)

Ultimately our decision to become a Christian and a servant for Jesus Christ boils down to faith. We have to make a choice that the Bible is the perfect word of God and that Jesus is the only way to Heaven. Faith in God is critical.

And without faith it is impossible to please God, because anyone who comes to him must believe that he exists, and that he rewards those who earnestly seek him.

(Hebrews 11:6)

What is faith? Once again the Bible gives us the answer.

Now faith is being sure of what we hope for and certain of what we do not see.

(Hebrews 11:1)

That definition of faith indicates to me that faith boils down to trust. We trust that Jesus is exactly who He said He was. Since we trust Him then we can also be certain that the promises He makes in the Bible are true. The disciples made a somewhat surprising request to Jesus one day. They had witnessed Jesus perform countless miracles so you would think their faith in Him would be strong. But notice what they wanted from Jesus.

The apostles said to the Lord, "Increase our faith!"

(Luke 17:5)

They made that request right after Jesus had told them about forgiving someone seven times in a day if the person repents and asks for forgiveness. I think the disciples realized that Jesus would actually do that. However, they knew they would not be able to forgive like that. Therefore, they wanted their faith in Jesus to increase so that their actions would be a greater reflection of Jesus.

One day a father brought his son to Jesus because his son was experiencing severe convulsions.

Jesus asked the boy's father, "How long has he been like this?" "From childhood," he answered. "It has often thrown him into fire or water to kill him. But if you can do anything, take pity on us and help us." "If you can?" said Jesus. "Everything is possible for him who believes." Immediately the boy's father exclaimed, "I do believe; help me overcome my unbelief!"

(Mark 9:21-24)

I think every Christian can relate to the father. He said I believe but then requested that Jesus help him overcome his unbelief which seems like such a contradiction. He realized that he wanted to believe, but he also knew he had some uncertainty about whether Jesus could actually heal his son. If he truly believed that Jesus could heal his son, would he not have asked, "If you would?" instead of "If you can?" He wanted Jesus to help him overcome that doubt. I really do not think he was saying if you heal my son then I will believe. I think at that moment he just realized that his faith was in fact weak, that he was not really sure that Jesus could heal his son, and his faith needed to be strengthened.

If you tell someone that you have faith in them to do the right thing it is because you know them and their character. They have proven to you by their past actions that they are someone who strives to be honest and that they are a person of integrity. That type of faith in someone can only be developed by having a close relationship with them. Ultimately, Christianity is about having a relationship with Jesus Christ. Being a Christian does involve serving Christ, but it is so much more. I love the following verses because Jesus points out that His believers are not just His servants, we are His friends.

> "I have told you this so that my joy may be in you and that your joy may be complete. My command is this: Love each other as I have loved you. Greater love has no one than this, that he lay down his life for his friends. You are my friends if you do what I command. I no longer call you servants, because a servant does not know his master's business. Instead, I have called you friends, for everything that I have learned from my Father I have made known to you. You did not choose me, but I chose you and appointed you to go and bear fruit–fruit that will last. Then the Father will give you whatever you ask in my name. This is my command: Love each other."
>
> (John 15: 11–17)

My hope at this point is you have decided that you do want to find out the truth about Jesus. Below are the steps I would recommend:

Simply pray to God that you desire to know the truth about Jesus. It may be that you have never really prayed to God before and you are not really sure what to say. Just say whatever you are feeling by expressing your desire to know the truth and the doubts and fears you may have. God loves a genuine and sincere heart that reaches out to Him.

Start reading the Bible. I would recommend starting with the four gospels, which are first four books of the New Testament: Matthew, Mark, Luke, and John. These four books detail Jesus' ministry on Earth and are filled with His teachings. I would also highly recommend that you get a good study Bible. A study Bible is simply one that helps explain the meaning and significance of scripture. It will help link Old Testament prophesy about Jesus and the fulfillment of that prophesy in the New Testament. I have used a great deal of scripture in this book that hopefully reveals the power of God's word and makes you want to learn more. Please realize the scripture that I have covered is only a small fraction of God's truths and wisdom that can be discovered in the Bible.

Reveal to a Christian friend what you are feeling and ask for them to be praying for you as you start your journey. I doubt seriously if you purchased this book on your own. Likely a Christian friend who obviously cares a great deal about you gave you this book to read.

Start attending a Christ centered church. It could be the church of the friend that introduced you to this book. One of your prayers to God could be for Him to lead you to the church He wants you to attend. I realize this will probably be the most difficult step because it involves doing something in public. It will be especially difficult and intimidating if you have never attended a church before. Just realize it is important to listen to God's word being preached and to be around other Christians. Like everything else we attempt in life, the first time is usually the hardest and most awkward.

Keep praying and reading the Bible. The only way to develop a relationship with Christ is to spend time with Him so that you can begin to truly know Him. The key is to prioritize some time every day for praying and reading.

If you are not a Christian and you have read this

book, I truly believe it is no coincidence that you have read this book at this moment in your life. The title of this book is *Please Seek the Truth*. The key to seeking the truth about Jesus is listening to the call of God. Notice that the steps outlined above ultimately involve us listening to God. When we pray, God will move in our hearts to teach us things. He speaks to us as we read His word. He can speak to us through other people.

Once you feel in your heart that you need to accept Christ's forgiveness and the gift of salvation, do not delay. I felt that need in my heart for several months before I accepted Christ and I realize now how foolish I was to wait.

Please be aware that as you start to feel the need to accept Christ there will also be another voice that will be constantly talking to you as well. That voice will not be a friend. That voice will be Satan. Satan hates God and the number one way he wants to hurt God is by working to keep people from accepting Jesus Christ. He will be trying to convince you that you do not want or need to accept Christ. He may tell you that Christianity is just a lot of nonsense. He may tell you that you will make a fool of yourself and he will try to frighten you about the changes that will take place in your life. He may tell you that you could not live the Christian life. He may say you need to make some changes before you could even consider becoming a Christian. He may be saying that you are a good person and there is no way a good person like you would be sent to Hell by a loving God. He does not want you to understand that while God is a loving God, He is also a righteous God who cannot just turn a blind eye to your sins.

Satan was telling me a lot of those lies as I felt the need to accept Jesus. Other Christian friends have shared with me how Satan was also telling them similar things as they were being called by God. The bottom line is God wants you to accept Jesus Christ as Savior. You do not need to make any changes to accept Christ and there is absolutely no reason for you to think that God could not possibly want you. As soon as you feel the call of God, please accept Jesus right then. Don't hesitate and pay any attention to Satan's lies.

It may be possible that at this moment you already feel the need to accept Christ and you want to do it now. Remember you do not have to do anything in advance in order to accept Christ. If so, you can pray the following prayer:

Dear Lord Jesus, I know that I am a sinner and need Your forgiveness. I believe that You died for my sins. I want to turn from my sins. I now invite You to come into my heart and life. I want to trust and follow You as Lord and Savior. In Jesus' name, Amen (Prayer copied from *Steps to Peace with God*)

If you really meant that prayer then you are now a Christian. Remember you have been born again and now you need to grow up in Christ. You need to start praying, reading the Bible, join a Christ centered church, follow in believer's baptism, and serving the Lord Jesus. Seek out what God's specific purpose is for your life and then experience the joy of fulfilling that purpose.

I would like to end by pointing out a very special

promise Jesus makes to us that summarizes the theme of this book. God will be found when we seek Him.

> So I say to you: Ask and it will be given to you; seek and you will find; knock and the door will be opened to you. For everyone who asks receives; he who seeks finds; and to him who knocks, the door will be opened.

(Luke 11:9–10)

My sincere hope is at some point in your life you will be able to answer the question, "Who is Jesus to me?" with the following reply. "Jesus is my Savior, He is my Lord, and He is my friend."

REFERENCES

Billy Graham ministry publication. *Steps to peace with God.* World Wide Publications.

Blackaby, Henry T., and Claude V. King. *Experiencing God: Knowing and Doing the*

Will of God. Nashville, Tennessee: LifeWay Press, 1990.

Lucado, Max. *Just like Jesus.* Dallas, Texas: W Publishing Group, 1998.

Mumford, Bob. *The Agape Road: Journey to Intimacy with the Father.* Nashville, Tennessee: LifeWay Press, 2000.